Jinsha Archaeology

www.royalcollins.com

Jinsha Archaeology

Reappearance of the
Sun and Immortal Bird

Huang Jianhua

Translated by Wang Xiaomin

RC

Books Beyond Boundaries

ROYAL COLLINS

Jinsha Archaeology
Reappearance of the Sun and Immortal Bird

Huang Jianhua
Translated by Wang Xiaomin

First published in 2023 by Royal Collins Publishing Group Inc.
Groupe Publication Royal Collins Inc.
BKM Royalcollins Publishers Private Limited

Headquarters: 550-555 boul. René-Lévesque O Montréal (Québec) H2Z1B1 Canada
India office: 805 Hemkunt House, 8th Floor, Rajendra Place, New Delhi 110008

Original Chinese Edition © Chengdu Times Press Co., Ltd.

ISBN: 978-1-4878-1157-0

To find out more about our publications, please visit www.royalcollins.com.

Contents

————∞◇∞————

Preface

What is Tianfu culture? It is a culture that has emerged, developed, and prospered in the "land of abundance." Tianfu culture centers on Chengdu City or Chuanxi Plain. Therefore, in this sense, Tianfu culture is Chengdu culture or the tradition of Chengdu, which is the unique lifestyle of Chengdu formed over thousands of years. It is history, life or daily routine which goes deeply into our memory and runs in our blood. It is visible or invisible for it may be a habit of thinking, a way of acting, a sentiment, a view, a hobby, or a feature.

It is common for researchers to focus more on cities like Beijing and Shanghai, which have undergone dramatic changes in modern times. However, I have always believed that Chengdu is a better representative of Chinese cities. It is because located in the inland of China, Chengdu enjoys a more traditional culture and richer Chinese elements. Chengdu is a typical Chinese city which represents similar inland cities to show us a different urban landscape which is different from that of the coast cities in China.

Chengdu Plain is rich in resources, which guarantees the development of Chengdu's economy and shapes a unique Tianfu material culture as well. The history of Tianfu culture can be traced back to the Ancient Shu (Early Shang Dynasty–316 BC). Dujiangyan is an important cradle of Tianfu culture. It cultivated the innovative spirit of Tianfu culture, laid its material foundation, and developed rice agriculture in the Chuanxi Plain. For more than 2,000 years, it provided a solid material foundation for the "land of abundance" and promoted the integration of nature and human culture, agricultural civilization and urban civilization, native culture and foreign culture.

Tianfu culture, growing from the Chuanxi Plain, is integrated into people's lifestyle, which includes food, poetry, music, and entertainment … the Chuanxi Plain has a rich cultural heritage and has produced many talented people in various fields, including literature, politics, military, science and technology, and commerce. These talents have injected new vitality into Tianfu culture and promoted to its vigorous development. Meanwhile, Tianfu culture intermingles with other cultures, drawing on the essence of other cultures and making its own unique contribution to Chinese culture.

The prosperity of Tianfu culture lies in the unique environment and climate of the Chuanxi Plain, rich produce, and convenient transportation. Therefore, we should learn and value these conditions. In today's world, almost all the better built and developed cities are a sound combination of traditional culture and modern civilization, and their material economy goes hand in hand with the growth of the spiritual culture.

To know the past of a city is to better know its present; to know the present of a city is to build a better future for the city. In this historic and cultural city of China, many historical and cultural sites have been destroyed or even disappeared with the changes of time. Therefore, it is very important to preserve the memory of Tianfu culture, which is the unique mark of the city and presents a true, three-dimensional, and comprehensive image of the city.

To know a city, we could start with many angles, use different materials and focus on different topics. Chengdu Times Press selected ten out of more than 70 books on Tianfu culture to be reprinted as the Tianfu culture city series. These ten books basically cover all aspects of Tianfu culture from ancient times to the present day, which include ancient civilization, cultural relics and archaeology, literature and poetry, and daily life.

In my opinion, it is a very good practice, which provides favorable conditions for these books to be brought back into the limelight. The introduction and research on Shu civilization, Tianfu culture and Chengdu provided by this set of books are helpful for us to understand the city and its culture, and it makes a great contribution to the study of the city as well. In the writing of these books, local scholars in Chengdu played a major role. They applied themselves to collecting information, conducting fieldwork, and trying hard to explore and find out the past of the city. They not only show the rich culture and history of the city but also provide precious information and spiritual nourishment for readers who are interested in Tianfu culture.

Wang Di
July 2, 2021

Foreword

———◦◇◇◦◦———

In the romantic poems of the Tang Dynasty (AD 618–907), the legendary Ancient Shu civilization, which suddenly disappeared, remains elusive and even mysterious. Those imaginative narrations and descriptions often arouse the infinite thoughts of later readers. In fact, as early as the Han (202 BC–AD 220) and Jin (AD 266–420) dynasties, a number of writings by literati and scholars have traced the history of Ancient Shu, such as *History of the Kings of Shu* by Yang Xiong and *Records of the Huayang Kingdom* by Chang Qu, which are well-known and highly cited. It goes without saying, however, that the Han and Jin dynasties Yang Xiong and Chang Qu lived are quite far away from the annihilated Ancient Shu, and their works are more speculative. Apart from these, we have no further documentation to rely on. Perhaps the *Classic of Mountains and Seas* compiled in the Warring States period (476 BC–AD 221) is an exception. According to Mr. Meng Wentong, a large part of the book was written by the Shu people. However, its strong mythological overtones suggest that it is not a credible history. In addition, its contents are too broad, for it covers almost the whole of the world. The Ancient Shu civilization was suddenly obliterated, and there was nothing left. The oracle bone inscriptions were left in the ruins of the Yin-Shang Dynasty (1300–1046 BC) for later scholars to excavate and interpret; however, nothing in the Ancient Shu remained, except the retrospection of later scholars, which is a great pity. No wonder people in modern times use the phrase "the mystery of Bashu" to describe it.

People who are used to getting to the bottom of matters find it hard to be satisfied with this self-prevarication. For a long time, people have been eager to uncover the mystery of Bashu and find out what the legendary Ancient Shu was all about. Those who are keen to do this include not only literati and scholars but also "fans" in many research fields and enthusiasts of literature and history. Professional and amateur research and exploration seem to have continued unabated, especially since the early 20th century. Without later archaeological discoveries, it would have been difficult to go beyond the research of previous generations, and such explorations would have remained in the realm of conjecture and speculation. Luckily for academic circles in 1986 and 2001, the world held its breath with the stunning discoveries of the Sanxingdui site in Guanghan and the Jinsha site in Chengdu. If nothing else, the mere fact that the whole world was watching and talking about them would suffice to go down in history.

Annihilation is chance, and discovery is also chance. When chances collide in time and space, an unexpected shock is sure to occur.

Lots of ancient nations in the world have created myriad and splendid cultures in the long course of historical development. In the ancient East, the Shu people located in the inland basin of the upper reaches of the Yangtze River also created a brilliant bronze civilization. It was once said that Sanxingdui site in Guanghan is a treasured land; in fact, the Jinsha site in Chengdu is not less important than the Sanxingdui site or even marginally more important than it.

The excavated materials demonstrate that the distinctive Ancient Shu civilization, represented by the Sanxingdui and Jinsha sites, is not simply a material form but also a manifestation of spiritual culture. However, we knew so little about it in the past. We should be grateful for the archaeological discoveries which have made up for the lack of documentary record and provided us with an opportunity to travel freely through time and space to trace the lost history, to find the ancient capital, to interpret the brilliant civilization, and to feel the timeless charm that causes spiritual shock.

Now, let's start with archaeological discoveries to unravel the mysteries that have long shrouded Ancient Shu civilization.

1

───◦◦◇◦◦───

Lost Civilization Unveiled by Archaeologists

In the spring of 2001, a great deal of ivory fragments and jade artifacts were unearthed in Jinsha Village, Supo Township, Chengdu City. Thus the Jinsha site was present at the stage of archaeology.

For both ancestors and modern people, the loss of a long and splendid civilization due to unexpected changes is a huge shame. The distinction lies in that the former was a feeling of helplessness, while the latter is nostalgia, while the latter cherished the memory of those times. However, as the downfall of a glorious era, the helplessness of the ancestors passed away and turned to dust and ashes. Without the amazing discoveries underground, the facts of ancient times would have been only a hazy legend for us. Fortunately, the archaeological discovery has built a bridge between the ancient and modern worlds, making it possible for us to experience our deep nostalgia.

From modern times to the contemporary era, most archaeological finds have been accidental, such as the best-known oracle bone inscriptions and the treasures in the Dunhuang Sutra Cave. In 1899, Wang Yirong, the head of the Imperial Academy in Beijing, discovered a Shang Dynasty (Yin-Shang Dynasty) divination inscribed on a "dragon bone" (a kind of large fossil mammal bone) when he went to Renda Chinese Medicine Shop for his malaria at Caishikou, outside the Xuanwumen. In1900, when spring was turning into summer, Wang Yuanlu, a Taoist, stationed at the Mogao Caves in Dunhuang, discovered a large number of scriptures scrolls and paintings when he cleaned sand in a secret cache. These accidental discoveries have had a profound impact on the academic field for over a century, and today oracle bone study and Dunhuang study have become predominant schools in the Orient, attracting many scholars from home and abroad to participate in their research.

Also, the discovery of the Sanxingdui and Yueliangwan ruins in Guanghan, Sichuan, was also by chance. According to *Cultural History of Ancient Sichuan* by Zheng Dekun, in the spring of 1931, Yan Daocheng, a local resident, accidentally found a large number of antiques, such as jade and stone disks and rings, when he dredged the stream. In the winter of 1933, Ge Weihan, an American professor and the curator of the Huaxi University Museum, tracked them down with his subordinate Li Mingjun and carried out the first archaeological excavation at Yueliangwan the following year, which attracted the attention of Guo Moruo, who lived in Japan. After a long period of waiting and anticipation, in 1986, at the end of summer, the amazing discovery of pits No. 1 and No. 2 in Sanxingdui was made by local brick factory workers who took soil to make bricks. The number of cultural relics from the two pits was marvelous in archaeological history as well as for their exquisiteness and cultural richness.

From a worldwide perspective, at the end of the 19th century, German archaeologist Schliemann excavated the ruins of ancient Troy at Hissaric

ABOVE LEFT Boat-shape coffins and tree-trunk coffins unearthed at Chengdu Commercial Street
ABOVE RIGHT Boat-shape coffins at the Chengdu Commercial Street site

Sanxingdui Museum on the Bank of Duck River

on the coast of the Asia Minor Peninsula. Right behind him, the British scholar Ivens discovered significant ancient cultural sites in Crete. These archaeological finds, intertwined with Homeric Hymns, have told us about the ancient Greek civilization.

Since the 20th century, major marvelous discoveries in Chinese archaeology have astonished the world, such as the Hongshan Culture relic in Liaoning; the Liangzhu Culture relics in Jiangsu and Zhejiang; the Yin Ruins in Anyang, Henan; the Terracotta Army at the Mausoleum of Qin Shi Huang in Lintong, Shaanxi; the tomb of Zeng Houyi in Hubei; the Han tomb at Mawangdui in Changsha; and the Underground Palace at Famen Temple in Shaanxi. They all have told us about the long and splendid Chinese civilization beyond time and space.

Many major archaeological discoveries in Chengdu were also fortuitous. For example, when the Sichuan provincial party committee canteen in Chengdu Commercial Street was built, a boat-shaped coffin and a tree-trunk coffin group were discovered. The site, a large tomb from the Kaiming Dynasty (Late Ancient Shu) of the Warring States period, has provided great number of resources to enable us to study the history, culture, and vicissitudes of the Ancient Shu state. Going forward, the site was approved by the State Council as a National Key Cultural Relics Protection Unit; moreover, a museum named after the site has become an important window to showcase the splendid culture of the Ancient Shu Kingdom.

The discovery of the Jinsha site was also a great coincidence. In the spring of 2001, a great deal of ivory fragments and jade artifacts were unearthed when a real estate company was working on a road project in Jinsha Village, Supo Township, Chengdu. Thus, the Jinsha site was present at the stage of archaeology.

Archaeologists took great patience in cleaning up the excavation site and sifted through the clay for many days. Luckily, more than 1,300 previous cultural antiques were cleaned, including gold, jade, bronze, stone, ivory, and bone articles. Among them, there were more than 30 articles made of gold, about 500 made of jade, and more than 250 pieces made of stone. These excavated artifacts are both numerous and exquisite. For example, among the gold objects, there are the Sun and Immortal Birds Gold Ornament, a human-face mask, a crown band, and a frog-shape foil; among the jade objects, there are heads, cong with divine faces, ax-shaped objects with animal faces, seashells, and plates; among the stone objects, there are kneeling human figure, tigers and snakes; among the bronze objects, there are human figures, birds, a bull's head, animal faces and collared engraving of three birds, etc. Their unique and vivid shapes, exquisite and superb handicraft, profound cultural connotations, and gorgeous artistic charm are breathtaking.

There is no doubt that the excavation of the Jinsha site, with extraordinary significance in unwinding the mystery of Ancient Shu history and culture, marks another major archaeological discovery after Sanxingdui. When the news was reported by the press, it immediately attracted widespread attention both at home and abroad, and indisputably won itself the title of one of the "Top Ten Archaeological Discoveries of 2001."

Formal excavation started after emergent cleaning. To accurately clear the relic's era and cultural background, the stratigraphic relationships and artifact features cannot be ignored, which are the most important conditions in archaeology. In the process of cleaning the relic, one of the most regrettable aspects was that the large digger not only severely damaged the antiques but also made the strata mixed, which posed great difficulties in sorting and researching the unearthed artifacts.

To clarify the stratigraphy and chronology of the site, archaeologists started scientific excavations from the top to bottom near the deep ditch dug by the digger. The area was rich in underground cultural deposits, with numbers of bronze and jade artifacts unearthed in the sixth stratum and an even greater number of jade and bronze artifacts in the seventh stratum, accompanied by a large quantity of ivory. This condition was rare compared with other Ancient Shu relics in the Chengdu Plain over the years. Based on the experience of field archaeologists, this site was presumably part of the whole relic. In the following excavations, more discoveries were explored, confirming that the archaeologists' intuition and judgment were accurate.

In the spring and summer of 2001, archaeologists mainly cleaned and explored the spot of the Jinsha site and its surroundings (the northeast corner of Meiyuan in Shufeng garden city). Numbers of antiques were unearthed here besides the ivory pits; plenty of pottery, jade, boar canines, deer horns, and stone artifacts were discovered at the northwestern of the excavation zone. By analyzing those unearthed antiques, archaeologists inferred that the ruin, covering about 300 m², may relate to the sacrificial activities of the Ancient Shu people. Moreover, the southern zone, covering an area of about 300 m², also discovered many semi-finished stone artifacts such as stone zhang and stone bi placed at an angle and in layers. Furthermore, no workshops for making jade and stone tools were found, thus the amount of the semi-finished stone artifacts here has become confusing.

In the autumn of 2001, after the rainy season, archaeologists focused on "Lanyuan" and the "Sports Park" of Shufeng garden city. The archaeological excavation covered 100,000 m² with more than 800 exploration ditches, but the actual excavation coverage was about 16,000 m². These explorations and archaeological excavations have played an important role in revealing the entire distribution of the Jinsha site and the state of the underground remains.

A few of the major large-scale archaeological excavation sites should be highlighted. In terms of location, Lanyuan is in the mid-south of the Jinsha site and covers an area of about 160,000 m², of which nearly 20,000 m² were

ABOVE Bronzewares unearthed at the Jinsha site

LEFT Jade wares unearthed at the Jinsha site

Meiyuan site

excavated, revealing the remains of a large number of houses with wooden bones and mud walls, rows of circular cellars, more than 400 ash pits, more than 90 burials, and the remains of three small steamed-bread-shape cellars. Moreover, pottery was unearthed, such as long-necked jars, high-handled beans, small flat-bottomed jars, earthenware bottles, etc. Some of them, such as rim jars, pointed-bottomed jars, and pointed-bottomed cups, are identical to antiques unearthed in Shi'erqiao in their features. In addition, some pottery, such as flat pots and high-handled cup-shaped vessels, as well as a small number of jade and stone vessels, bronze vessels, and gold vessels, were also excavated. According to the stratigraphic relationship and the genre of the unearthed antiques, it can be inferred that the cultural remains can be dated from the late Shang Dynasty to the early Western Zhou Dynasty (1045–771 BC); more specifically, that would be the site of a residential area and burial ground of Ancient Shu people.

The Sports Park is in the middle of the Jinsha site, and to the north and the east are Lanyuan and Meiyuan respectively, covering an area of about 90,000 m². After more precise exploration, the distribution of cultural deposits was confirmed as being over an area of about 36,000 m². In the zone, the archaeologist found many remains of houses and 15 burials, most of which were relocated. In addition, a small number of jade and stone tools and pottery were unearthed, which can be dated to the early Western Zhou Dynasty. It is speculated that the area may have been the residential quarters of the Ancient Shu people, but it may be abandoned for some reason and turned into a cemetery later.

Sanhe Garden site

Archaeologists have previously explored Sanhe Garden, Huangzhong Community (north of Jinsha site). Seventeen ancient houses and kilns, 13 tombs, and more than 300 ash pits were discovered; in particular, a group of special architectural remains of a large-scale and regular layout was inferred so that it may be a part of the palace of the Ancient Shu ruling class by combining the whole exploration.

Taking an overall view of the scale and layout of these functional divisions, as well as the numerous architectural remains and numbers of excavated artifacts, it could be seen that the Jinsha site was by no means an ordinary site but probably a capital of the ancient state of Shu during the Shang and Zhou (1046–256 BC) periods.

The history of city building by the Shu people can be traced back to the late Neolithic period (10000–4500 BC). Six ancient cities of earlier Baodun culture and Sanxingdui had been found in Chengdu Plain. Archaeological data showed that the earlier cities of Ancient Shu were small in scale but expanded later. In the earliest period, they settled their homes on the northwestern edge of the Minshan Mountain, then gradually built along the terraces on both sides of the Minjiang River tributaries toward the heart of the plain.

The Mangcheng site, for example, is located about 12 km south of Dujiangyan on the western edge of the Chengdu Plain, and at the upper reaches of the ancient riverway of Wenjingjiang, covering an area of 105,000 m². With a square layout, the site has two inner and outer rings of rammed walls made of earth taken from the ground and is probably the earliest city built by the Shu people when they emigrated from the Minshan Mountain to the Chengdu Plain. Besides, the ancient city ruins of Shuanghe and Zizhu in Chongzhou are similar to Mangcheng. The ancient city of Shuanghe is also divided into two layers, inside and outside, and is built on a rammed slope, covering an area of about 100,000 m², and is located at the confluence of the Weijiang and Pojiang rivers in the middle reaches of the Wenjingjiang river. The nearby ruins of the ancient city of Zizhu covered an area of about 200,000 m². The Wenjing River, also known as the Xihe River in ancient times, was also an important tributary of the Minjiang River flowing through the Chengdu Plain. Downstream at the point where the Xihe River is about to merge into the Minjiang River are the ruins of the ancient Xinjin Baodun, with a rectangular layout and rammed city walls, covering an area of over 600,000 m² and dating from around 4,500 years ago. Ancient Pixian ruins and Yufu ruins in Wenjiang are all of the same period as the ancient Baodun City, cover an area of 310,000 m² and 320,000 m² respectively, and have been the core zone of the Chengdu Plain.

These ancient ruins in the Chengdu Plain are not large in scale, lying in the fact that the human resources of the Ancient Shu were still lacking, and their production was still at a relatively simple and backward stage. Nonetheless, those ruins have shown the details about the development of Ancient Shu, that the Ancient Shu transferred from a primitively simple society to a sophisticated city with flood-resistant function. Going forward, these ruins suggested that the Ancient Shu stepped out of backwardness and ignorance and strode into prosperity. The sparks of early urban civilization appeared in the Chengdu Plain in those times.

In the Yin-Shang Dynasty, the Ancient Shu was much more prosperous with well-developed agriculture, and flourishing development on all fronts. The Shu people established a large-scale capital at Sanxingdui, creating a splendid and distinctive bronze culture. According to the archaeological excavations, the total area of Sanxingdui is about 2.6 km², and the human and material resources had huge development compared with the early ancient sites of the Baodun culture. As the core capital of the Ancient Shu, Sanxingdui had become an important center of civilization in the upper reaches of the Yangtze River due to its prominence in religious, political, economic, and cultural aspects.

Sport Park site

The amount of unearthed antiques in Sanxingdui showed encyclopaedical cultural connotations, which fully corroborated the records in the ancient literature and showed that the legendary ancient Kingdom of Shu was not fiction. More importantly, it shows that the Minjiang River valley was also one of the cradles of Chinese civilization, with its culture as long and developed as that of Central China and other regions. But the splendid Ancient Shu civilization seemly vanished without any signs, with the glorious Sanxingdui City abandoned too. The disappearance of Sanxingdui was still an enigma. Besides, the whereabouts of vanished ancient civilization has also confused us.

The important discoveries in Jinsha gave us more knowledge about this disappeared civilization. The explored area is in the western part of Chengdu, just 38 km north of the Sanxingdui site in Guanghan, covering about three km² and is indeed large. The geographical condition of the entire site is flat with numbers of rivers alongside. For example, the ancient Pi Riverway is in the north, the Qingshui River in the south, and the middle is the Modi River across from west to east, which is in accordance with the traditional city-building style of the Ancient Shu people who set up the city in terms of the direction of the stream and the nearby terrain features, all of which showed the characteristics of living by rivers. The Jinsha site is not only large in scale but also has a clear layout: live quarters, a burial ground, a palace for the ruling class and religious areas, as well as workshops for pottery production, kiln making, jade, and stone. It was worth noting that numbers of sites from the Shang and Zhou dynasties have been discovered in recent years along both sides of the river in a continuous west-to-east distribution over an area of about 10 km. In terms of chronology, the Jinsha site is contiguous with, and slightly later than, the Sanxingdui site. In terms of the overall scale and layout, the Jinsha site is vaster than ancient Sanxingdui, and the number and ranking of excavated artifacts, as well as their exquisiteness, are never inferior to those of Sanxingdui. It is clear that there is a very close relationship between the Jinsha site and Sanxingdui. If the ancient Sanxingdui City was the capital of the Ancient Shu Kingdom in the era of Yu Fu and Du Yu, was it possible that the Jinsha site was the capital of the Ancient Shu Kingdom in the Kai Ming era?

Although the Jinsha site has not yet been discovered to be the capital of the Ancient Shu Kingdom, it is indisputable that the Jinsha site, with its prosperous settlements and magnificent scale, was the precursor to the establishment of the Ancient Shu Dynasty (Early Shang Dynasty–316 BC) in Chengdu area. It would be an appropriate analogy to call the Jinsha site the "mother city" of Chengdu.

Ancient Shu was blessed with unique natural conditions; thus, the Shu people congregated around rivers and took advantage of natural resources. The rivers fed the Shu people, irrigated their fields, provided access to connect with the outside, and offered them abundant resources for fishing, all of which were closely related to the life of the Shu people. The Yu Fu clan, in the historical legends of Ancient Shu, was a tribe that was good at fishing. In 1200 to 500 BC, with Duyu who taught farmers to do farming, and Bieling who made great achievements in controlling and preventing floods, agriculture in those times was well-developed, as neither fishing nor rice farming could be developed without abundant water. The numerous rivers provided great convenience for the people, but the riverside cities were prone to suffer a lot when floods came, and other natural disasters happened. In the earlier Baodun culture, the sloping ramparts, with no gates, embodied the Ancient Shu people's awareness of flood control. Besides the regime change between the dynasties of the Ancient Shu Kingdom, the destruction of ancient Sanxingdui City may also have been caused by flooding disasters across the city.

After the sudden annihilation of the Sanxingdui civilization, Jinsha became increasingly prosperous and blossomed at that time, even probably replacing the status of Sanxingdui, the capital city of the Ancient Shu Kingdom. It should be noticed that the Jinsha site was not a city that appeared suddenly. On the contrary, it had undergone a long period of taking shape, reaching its peak, and moving into thriving and becoming prosperous. The earliest inhabitants of the Jinsha Ruins may have been another clan or tribe of Ancient Shu people, rather than migrants from Sanxingdui after it was destroyed. During the Shang and Zhou dynasties, many of these Ancient Shu clans or tribes probably inhabited the Chengdu Plain, and they allied with each other, forming the Kingdom of Ancient Shu. Over the long course of history, when one prominent clan or tribe in Ancient Shu went into decline, another one would gradually flourish. The strength and weakness of these clans and tribes did a lot to the vicissitudes of the Shu Kingdom. However, such an irreversible trend led to the decline and even the oblivion of the Sanxingdui civilization, with the ever-increasingly prosperous Jinsha civilization playing a substitute role.

2

——◦◦◇◦◦——

What Ivory Reveals

The Central Plains peoples and the Ancient Shu people were nostalgic for the herds of elephants, hence the character "想象" (imagination). The elephant herds that migrated south left unforgettable memories, imagination for our ancestors, and a wealth of inspiration for future generations.

When archaeologists entered the site to start the cleaning work, they found a large number of ivory fragments, followed by the damaged pit with stacked ivories. Through careful excavation and cleaning, it could be clearly observed that eight layers of ivory were in the pit, and many jade and bronze wares were placed at the bottom and wall of the pit. These stacked ivories are large. Most are more than one meter long, and the largest was 150 cm long. The delicate luster of the ivories is still visible, even though they had been buried for thousands of years. After careful consideration, the archaeologists were not in such a rush to take the ivories out of the pit. Still, they protected them according to the conditions of the pit to prevent possible dehydration and cracking of large quantities of ivory once excavated. It was only when the excavation work ended that the ivories were gradually taken out and sealed for preservation. Judging from the stratigraphic relations and the type of excavated relics, the pit dated back to the early Western Zhou Dynasty (1046–771 BC), to the early Spring and Autumn Period (770–476 BC), and is probably related to the religious activities of the Ancient Shu people.

LEFT Jade tablet with its line drawing from pit No. 2 at the Sanxingdui site

ABOVE Ivories from pit No. 2 at the Sanxingdui site

So far, according to preliminary statistics from the archaeologists, more than 1,000 ivory tusks have been unearthed from the Jinsha site. The sheer number is amazing. Large areas of wild boar tusks and antlers were also found in the nearby excavation site. Preliminary identification shows that the wild boar tusks are all lower canines, which may not be random, but specially selected. These are all very intriguing phenomena. According to the archaeological excavation data in the Sichuan Basin and the surrounding areas, in the early autumn of 1986, 13 ivories were unearthed in the pit No. 1 of Sanxingdui, and 67 ivories were unearthed in the pit No. 2, which were generally 80–120 cm long. Moreover, 120 pieces of ivory beads and fragments of ivory carvings were also in the pit No. 2. In the tombs of the Daxi cultural site in Wushan County, people also excavated ivories and ivory products, such as ivory bracelets and ornaments. There are also many similar archaeological discoveries in other areas, such as an ivory carving with a pattern of two birds facing the sun unearthed at the Hemudu cultural site, ivory carvings unearthed at the tombs of the Dawenkou cultural site in Shandong Province, and ivory products unearthed at the Yin Ruins in Anyang, Henan Province. According to these materials, it is a common phenomenon that a small number of ivory and ivory products were unearthed from the site of the Neolithic Age to the Shang and Zhou dynasties. Such a large amount of ivory unearthed at the Jinsha site is a rare wonder in the history of Chinese archaeology and even in the history of world archaeology. Why did the Ancient Shu people who inhabited the Jinsha site in the Shang and Zhou dynasties have so many ivories? Where did these ivories come from? How did they get them? For what purpose? These are all problems that need to be explored and solved.

Let's start with the use of the ivories. Scholars have researched the ivories unearthed from the Sanxingdui site, and most think they are sacrificial articles of the Ancient Shu. For example, the large bronze standing figures with their exaggerated hands in the shape of rings are probably holding ivory—a sacrificial object used in large rituals. The patterns of jade zhang unearthed in Sanxingdui site provide a graphic depiction of the use of ivories. The thick, curved, pointed object suspended inside the sacred mountain on the left is almost identical to the actual ivory, which vividly illustrates the Ancient Shu's custom of using ivory in grand rituals. According to relevant records of the documents handed down from ancient times, the ancients had many sacrificial forms. For example, in the *Rites of Zhou Dynasty*, there was a description of "Using jade zhang and dishe (an ancient type of jade) to worship mountains and rivers." In the *Comprehensive Manual*, sacrificial offerings are buried underground when people worship the mountains and forests; while they worship the rivers and lakes, offerings are submerged underwater. These sacrificial activities prevailed in the Central Plains during the Western Zhou Dynasty. Referring to the scene carved on the jade zhang of Sanxingdui site, it can be seen that the same ways were used when the Ancient Shu people sacrificed at the sacred mountain. However, the Ancient Shu people not only used jade zhang but also hung ivory, which showed that some of the characteristics of the Ancient Shu differed from those in the central Plains.

A broken jade zhang with patterns was also unearthed at the Jinsha site. The pattern is divided into two parts. It clearly depicts a man kneeling sideways and carrying a curved ivory tusk on his shoulder. It may be a real scene of the Ancient Shu people offering ivory during their sacrificial activities. In the Central Plains and other regions, ivories are usually carved into ivory products. For example, many ivory products have been excavated in the Yin Ruins. They are rich in shape with exquisite carvings. According to the unearthed objects, most of the ivory carvings of the Shang Dynasty were practical objects of the aristocracy and later became burial articles of the deceased. Although some ivory products have also been found at the Sanxingdui site and the Jinsha site, the Ancient Shu people may have preferred to use ivory in sacrificial activities, especially ivory and jade zhang as sacrifices to the sacred mountain, which may have been a special custom.

It is worth identifying: what is the secret of this love for ivory? It is known that the elephant is a land mammal animal of great size in nature, which is also fierce and intelligent. It has had a friendly relationship with human beings since ancient times. In addition, ivory has a texture similar to that of fine jade and a white and delicate color, so it was regarded as a spiritual object by the ancients. It is probably because of this reason, and in addition, the sacrificial activities in the Ancient Shu period were particularly prosperous, so the Ancient Shu people compared the large amount of ivory they obtained with the "jade presented to god" and used it as a sacrificial object for the gods, mountains, and rivers.

Broken jade zhang blade with a man kneeling sideways and carrying a curved ivory tusk on his shoulder

Second, the source of these ivories is also a question worth exploring. The ivory unearthed at the Sanxingdui site has been identified as an Asian elephant, and the seashells unearthed at the same time have been identified as cowrie shells, cypraeatigris, and monetaria annulus, all of which lived in the warm waters of the Pacific and Indian oceans. Some scholars believe that the seashells and ivory unearthed at Sanxingdui site are probably from foreign countries, related to the long-distance business activities and cultural exchanges in the Ancient Shu. In some previous works, I also thought that the

Ivory cup from the tomb of Fuhao

ivory and seashells unearthed at Sanxingdui site were imported products, which might come from Dianmian, South Asia, and India.

The Jinsha site has unearthed a larger amount of ivory. The source of these ivories cannot but arouse our new scrutiny and thinking. The ivory unearthed at the Jinsha site has been identified as an Asian elephant. It is known that only male Asian elephants have front teeth (ivory), and each male elephant has two front teeth. There are more than 1,000 ivories unearthed from the Jinsha site, which must have been taken from more than 500 male elephants. Judging from the length of the ivories, many of them are adult elephants, which would be a huge elephant group of an astonishing number. If more than 1,000 ivories, weighing several tons, come from a distant foreign country, obtaining and transporting them is a relatively big problem. Then, was there an elephant group in the Sichuan Basin during the Shang and Zhou dynasties? At that time, the Chengdu Plain with luxuriant trees and abundant water and grass would not have been an important habitat for a large number of elephants. Are these amazing amounts of ivory obtained from the elephants that haunt the area? Since no elephant remains have been found, this can only be a guess at present. However, this possibility should exist from the information disclosed by various documents and archaeological materials.

In the literature of pre-Qin times, there are many records about elephants. For example, in *Master Lü's Spring and Autumn Annals · Ancient Music*, there is a description of "the Shang people tamed the elephants and did evil at Dongyi (people living in the lower reaches of the Yellow River Basin), so the Duke of Zhou led the army to expel them to the south of the Yangtze River." Scholars generally believe that the Shang people tamed elephants to fight a war. As for the "Shang people," some people think that they are Yin people, while others think that they should be southerners, so there is a saying that the Duke of Zhou sent troops to drive them away. Although the explanations are different, the taming of elephants by the Yin people is probably a historical situation that did exist. According to the archaeological

Bronze elephant statue of the Shang Dynasty unearthed in Liling, Hunan Province

Bronze elephant statue of the Western Zhou Dynasty unearthed at the Yu Country tomb in Baoji City, Shaanxi Province

Elephant, phoenix, and deer painted on the picture stone of Han Dynasty

Picture of "Elephant Taming" painted on the picture stone of Han Dynasty

data, the oracle bone inscriptions unearthed in the Yin Ruins often see the word "象" (elephant), phrases "获象" (obtaining an elephant), and "来象" (coming to an elephant). The character "象" is characterized by a long nose and huge teeth, which indicates that the Yin people were very familiar with elephants, so there are such lifelike pictographs.

Elephant pits were found in the Yin Ruins, where adult elephants and young elephants were buried. Lifelike jade statues of elephant and various ivory products were unearthed from the tomb of Fu Hao. All these are evidence that elephants once existed in the Central Plains of the Yellow River Basin during the Yin-Shang Dynasty. There are also some ancient geographical names related to elephants, such as 豫州 (Yuzhou) in *Yu Gong*.

FAR LEFT Bronze figure wearing an animal-shaped mitre at pit No. 2 at the Sanxingdui site

LEFT Bronze bat with a long nose and three-dimensional elephant head in Shang and Zhou dynasties unearthed in ZhuWa Street, Mengyang Town, Pengxian County

In this name, "豫" (Alias of Henan) is the combination of "象" and "邑" (city), which shows that Henan was once an area producing elephants in the Yin-Shang Dynasty. According to the investigations of Luo Zhenyu, Wang Guowei and Xu Zhongshu, the climate in the Central Plains during the Yin-Shang Dynasty was warm and suitable for the survival of rhinoceros and elephants. After that, the climate turned cold, and the rhinoceros and elephants gradually moved south. As famous scholars in modern times, their analysis and views are indeed very insightful.

In ancient China, elephants enjoyed a vast area to live and multiply. In the *Book of Songs · Lu Song · Pan River*, there is a sentence: "The savage Huaiyi people have already submitted to our country and hurriedly come to offer treasures, such as genki, ivory, and copper produced in the south." The Huai Yi people took the ivory as a present, indicating that the Jiang Huai River Basin was once an area inhabited by elephants. In *Discourses of the States · Chu Yu*, there is a description "Can the horns and teeth of rhinoceros, yaks and elephants in Bapu be exhaustible?" According to the *Commentary of Zuo · the 4th Year of Duke Ding*, in the middle reaches of the Yangtze River, King Zhao of the Chu lost the battle with the troops of King Helu of Wu. When escaping the pursuit of the army of Wu, he tied a torch to the tail of the elephant, asked his subordinates to run to the Wu division, and was finally able to escape. This shows that the state of Chu once domesticated elephants, and only when it was in danger could it drive elephants to fight and achieve miraculous results. The *Classic of Mountains and Seas · the South of China* has

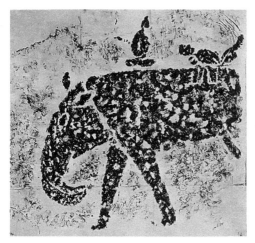

Picture of "Elephant Riding" on the picture stone of Han Dynasty in Tanghe, Henan Province

The archaeologists are cleaning the ivory excavation.

the saying "the python swallows the elephant"; the *Classic of Mountains and Seas · Mountains in the Center* says that "Min Mountain, where the river flows out … Many of its creatures are rhinoceros and elephants"; the *Records of the Huayang Kingdom · Records of Shu* also mentions that "Shu is a state because of the emperor … It has many treasures including jades … rhinoceros and elephants." It can be seen from this that, in ancient times, the upper reaches of the Yangtze River and the Sichuan Basin also had elephants. According to the environmental archaeological materials, the climate in the Yangtze River Basin and Sichuan Basin during the Shang and Zhou dynasties was warmer and more humid than in the Yellow River Basin and the Central Plains. This climate was more suitable for birds, beasts, and large animals, as it contained abundant rivers and luxuriant trees. At that time, the elephant was probably a very familiar animal to people in Chu and Bashu, and there was a very friendly relationship between people and elephants. Unearthed cultural relics in these areas have also proved this. For example, the bronze elephant statue from the Shang Dynasty unearthed in Liling, Hunan Province, has a long nose rolling up tightly and stout limbs, which is lifelike. It should be a true imitation of the elephant by the local producers. The elephant statue of the late Shang Dynasty unearthed at the Doujitai in Baoji City, Shaanxi Province, has a vivid and lifelike shape similar to that of the elephant statue in Liling, Hunan Province. A lifelike little elephant was carved on the cover of the statue. This precious cultural relic has been scattered overseas and is now collected in the flier Art Museum in Washington, USA. The bronze statue with an animal head unearthed from the pit No. 2 of Sanxingdui site, with an exaggerated and strange crown ornament, portrays the curled elephant trunk. At the same time, the bronze portrait with vertical eyes unearthed in pit No. 2, its cloud pattern above the nose, also makes people think of the curled elephant trunk, which is a symbolic expression full of imagination. In addition, among the bronze wares from Shang and Zhou dynasties unearthed in ZhuWa Street, Mengyang Town, Pengxian County, there is a bronze bat with a long nose and three-dimensional elephant head. Its head, long nose, and protruding ivory are also very lifelike. It is obvious that such familiarity can only be achieved by frequent contact with elephants. All these show that elephants were common animals in Shu during the Shang and Zhou dynasties.

If we link these documents and archaeological findings, we can see that the large number of ivories unearthed at the Jinsha site did not come from a distant foreign land, and they were likely produced in Ancient Shu or obtained from the habitat of elephants in the middle and upper reaches of the Yangtze River. Considering many wild boar tusks and antlers unearthed at the Jinsha site, it is obvious that they were hunted locally or nearby by the Ancient Shu people.

What a large amount of ivories reveal is rich information. They not only tell us about the origin of ivory but more importantly, expand our understanding of the ancient environment. Today, people's understanding of the ancient environment is often limited by the constraints of time and space. Even rigorous scholars are no exception, often inadvertently ignoring the environmental differences in different time and spaces. This difference and the change of the environment will always have a great impact on people's social life. The causes of environmental change are both natural and man-made. How people and the environment get along harmoniously has been a big problem, which has been worth thinking about since ancient times. As mentioned earlier, the climate change during the Yin-Shang Dynasty caused the gradual southward migration of elephants. Was it also affected by human factors?

What archaeological data tells us is that in the Shang and Zhou dynasties, the Sichuan Basin and the middle and upper reaches of the Yangtze River were likely to have had a large area of dense forest. The ship coffins and single-wood coffins unearthed in Chengdu Commercial Street might be made from materials produced in these areas. At that time, in addition to the luxuriant forests and the rice fields reclaimed by our ancestors, there were probably many swamps and wetlands with plenty of water and lush grass in the Chengdu Plain. This unique ecological condition naturally makes the place a paradise for all kinds of birds and animals and provided great convenience for the fishing and hunting activities of the Ancient Shu people. It should be mentioned here that there is a paragraph in the *Classic of Mountains and Seas · China*: "In the southwest where the black water flows, there is a place called Du Guangye, where Hou Ji is buried. It produces Gao Shu, Gao Dao, Gao Shu, and Gao Ji. All kinds of grains grow naturally and can be sown in winter and summer. The phoenix birds sing and dance freely, the Lingshou tree blooms and bears fruit, and the bushes and trees are luxuriant. There are also various birds and wild animals living in groups." According to the research of ancient and modern scholars such as Yang Shen, Yuan Ke, and Meng Wentong, it is believed that the "Du Guangye" is the Chengdu Plain. It can be seen from this description that there were many kinds and numbers of animals in Ancient Shu. According to archaeological materials, there were not only many birds, tigers, wild boars, deer, snakes, fish, and frogs, but also a large number of elephants. The Ancient Shu people living in this natural environment had created a brilliant bronze culture. They developed rice farming in the Shang and Zhou dynasties, but fishing and hunting activities were still important sidelines for them. The pattern of the gold stick unearthed at Sanxingdui site and the pattern of the gold crown belt unearthed at Jinsha site both highlight the theme of the long-rod feather arrow shooting through the bird's neck into the fish's body, which reveals that the Ancient Shu people were good at shooting fish and hunting birds and animals with feather arrows. In the hunting activities of the Ancient Shu people, wild boars and deer might have been the main quarry. A large number of wild boar tusks and antlers unearthed at the Jinsha site is the best evidence. Except that, in order to meet the needs of various sacrificial activities, it was likely that elephant herds were often hunted to obtain ivory. How can tons of ivory be obtained without hunting?

But there are also some questions. First, many cultural relics unearthed fully show the Ancient Shu people's respect for elephants. For example, they deliberately cast an elephant pattern on bronze sacrificial vessels or used

Boat-shaped coffins of the Ancient Shu from Chengdu Commercial Street

the elephant trunk as the crown or forehead decoration of the figure, which gives the elephant a special symbolic meaning. Would the Ancient Shu people with such special feelings and reverence make elephants targets for hunting? Moreover, elephants are very intelligent and fierce animals, making it difficult to hunt and kill hundreds of wild and untamed adult males living in the mountains and forests in the Shang and Zhou dynasties, when there were no advanced weapons. Second, the archaeological excavations in the Chengdu Plain and Sichuan Province have not found the remains that must be left after hunting elephants. So, how did people get the thousands of ivories unearthed at the Jinsha site? This is really a puzzling question. In fact, the truth is not complicated. If we understand the composition of the Ancient Shu people, the problem will be solved.

The literature and archaeological data tell us that the southwestern region upstream of the Yangtze River has been a multi-ethnic cohabitation since ancient times. The Ancient Shu was a kingdom formed by many clans and tribal alliances, mainly composed of the Ancient Shu people who lived on the Chengdu Plain, including many large and small tribes in the southwestern region and some clans or tribes that migrated from other surrounding areas. They all belonged to a large cultural system, with many common beliefs and spiritual pursuits, but they also had some different characteristics in traditional customs. The Ancient Shu culture showed strong inclusiveness and was full of vitality because of this. It was also due to the changes in the strong relationships between these tribes and clans that the

Vertical-eyed bronze mask from pit No. 2 of the Sanxingdui site

rise and fall of the successive dynasties in Ancient Shu history were formed. For example, Emperor Wang, Du Yu, who taught the people to farm, was rumored to have come from Jiangyuan and married Li of the Liang family from Zhuti (today's Zhaotong City, Yunnan Province). After becoming powerful through tribal alliances and developing agriculture, he replaced the Yufu tribe and became the king of Shu. Bie Ling, of the Kaiming tribe, came from Jingchu and, after entering Shu, was appointed by Du Yu as his prime minister. He gained control of the Shu kingdom by successfully managing floods and water disasters and replaced Du Yu with abdication to establish the Kaiming Dynasty. The ancient ancestors of the mid-Yangtze River region in Jingchu were prevalent in witchcraft and had customs of believing in and using ivory to ward off evil spirits. The *Rites of Zhou · Autumn Officer · Hu Zhuo Shi* says that by piercing ivory with elm wood and sinking it into the water, one can beat water monsters or drive away evil spirits. This kind of witchcraft against evil spirits may have been quite popular among the ancient tribes living by the banks of the mid-Yangtze River. The Kaiming tribe from Jingchu probably had a long-standing way and habit of hunting ivory. After they migrated to Shu, the Kaiming tribe and other tribes of the Ancient Shu Kingdom merged well, gradually became stronger after years of development, and gained the support of many tribes, finally becoming the rulers of Shu. In this process lasting for decades, the cultural characteristics of the Kaiming tribe and other tribes of the Ancient Shu Kingdom gradually became consistent. However, they may still have retained some traditional customs of their clan, such as frequently hunting elephants and using ivory extensively in sacrificial activities or witchcraft against evil spirits, which is a significant example.

From this perspective, could many ivories unearthed from the Jinsha site be related to the Kaiming Clan? Further speculation suggests that the Jinsha site may have been the early habitat of the Kaiming Clan before replacing the Du Yu Dynasty. Currently, more evidence and in-depth exploration are needed to conclude, but this possibility should exist. The *Annals of the Kings of Shu* states that after Bie Ling replaced Du Yu and established the Kaiming Dynasty, he set up Fanxiang as the capital city in Guangdu and only moved to Chengdu in the fifth generation of the Kaiping Dynasty. Before the fifth generation of the Kaiming Dynasty, the ancient capital was still in the capital of Du Yu. If we analyze it reasonably, it is unlikely that the Kaiming Clan, who came from Jingchu, immediately moved into the capital after migrating to Shu. They should have had another early habitat. The Jinsha site, which is 38 km away from the Sanxingdui site, is likely to be the early habitat of the Kaiming Clan after they migrated to Shu. After the Kaiming Clan became powerful and replaced Du Yu to establish a stable dynasty, they moved back to the Jinsha site as their foundation, making it the new capital.

The source of many ivories at the Jinsha site indicates that huge elephant herds were inhabiting the upper and middle reaches of the Yangtze River and the Sichuan Basin during the Shang and Zhou periods. Due to the need for witchcraft and sacrificial activities, the Ancient Shu people also made elephant herds their hunting targets. In addition to the possibility of human hunting, it cannot be ruled out that a sudden natural disaster led to the mass death of elephant herds, allowing the Ancient Shu people to obtain a shocking amount of ivory. This natural disaster may have been a severe flood or other uncontrollable natural disaster. According to historical records, a great flood occurred during the Du Yu era, and many places in Shu were submerged into a swamp. This endangered the Ancient Shu people's survival and perhaps led to the elephants' misfortune. In summary, it was a dual reason of humans and nature that led to the disappearance of elephant herds in the Yangtze River Basin and the Sichuan Basin. Due to the departure of the elephant herds, the Central Plains ethnic groups and the Ancient Shu people developed a sense of nostalgia, leading to the birth of the word "imagination." The original meaning of this word was to express the yearning for the object. The departure of the elephant herds that migrated south left unforgettable memories and imaginations for the ancestors and left abundant inspiration for future generations. How to better protect the environment and live in harmony with nature is a topic that is always worth pondering.

3

—◦◦◇◦◦—

Stories behind the Bronze Sculpture

When the rise and fall of dynasties became history, when all the wealth, joys, and sorrows turned to dust and ashes, only those extraordinary creations, which embodied the essence of civilization, still shone with brilliance.

The Ancient Shu people in the Shang and Zhou dynasties created splendid material and spiritual culture, especially in bronze statues, which were rare masterpieces in the history of Oriental Fine Arts. The numerous statues unearthed in the Sanxingdui pit No. 1 and pit No. 2 were all magical in their forms. These statues astonished the outside world with their glorious cultural connotations and various artistic features. There is nothing eternal and immortal in the world, but the glamour of culture and art can break through the limitation of time and space. When the rise and fall of dynasties became history, when all the wealth, joys, and sorrows turned to dust and ashes, only those extraordinary creations, which embodied the essence of civilization, still shone with brilliance and echoed in our minds beyond time and space. The Ancient Shu people immersed us fully in the glamour of the statues which were crystallized by their romantic imagination and extraordinary talent. The statues not only unfold a lively oriental civilization

Bronze human mask and its excavation from pit No. 2 of the Sanxingdui site

Small bronze human head from the Jinsha site

but also eloquently demonstrate the sacrificial activities and the social life of the Ancient Shu Kingdom. The presence of the bronze statues unearthed in the Sanxingdui was meaningful. They symbolized royal and divine power and the epitome of the ruling class formed by various tribal alliances in the Ancient Shu Kingdom. Besides the serious content, there may be many lost legends. The bronze statues unearthed at the Jinsha Ruins also have rich meanings and may hide many little-known stories.

Four hundred and seventy bronze objects have been put in order, accounting for more than a third of the total. However, only a few bronze figures have been excavated from the Jinsha site. At present, only one small bronze standing figure has been published, together with a small bronze head. The condition in Jinsha sets great difference compared with Sanxingdui, which puzzled us in that the latter has excavated more bronze figure statue groups than the former.

Bronze standing figure from the Jinsha site
(front and back)

Line drawings of the bronze standing
figure from the Jinsha site

Let's look at the bronze figure, which is made up of a standing figure and an insert. As the standing figure is 14.61 cm high and the insert 4.99 cm, the total height is 19.6 cm with the weight of 641 g. The casting process is similar to those excavated from the Sanxingdui site. According to the residual clay core of the model, it was cast after the mold was made, and then the statue was polished. The entire statue is modeled in a dignified upright position, with the standing figure wearing a strange ring-shaped crowned hat with 13 arc-shaped decorative crowns around the hat, resembling a bent ivory tusk distributed at equal distances, which easily reminds people of the flickering light of the sun.

This eerie and ethereal crown may have a special symbolic meaning. The face of the standing figure is relatively thin, with a serious expression, open eyes, and far-forward stare, and pierced earlobes on both the left and right. Behind his head, he wears a long three-stranded plait in parallel with a brass band tied around the bottom, trailing down to the hips. He is wearing a robe with a belt around his waist and a short staff-like object slung across his chest and belly, perhaps a ritual weapon. The feet, which do not show the toes, appear to be clad in footwear and stand on top of a *Ya*-shape (*Ya* is a Chinese character which is like the letter Y in shape in English) insert. It is worthy of noting that the arms of the standing figure are in a position of encircling the object, the left arm is bent at the elbow in front of the chest, the right arm is raised at shoulder level, and the hands are held in a seemly grip, with the hollowed fists facing each other in a diagonal line, suggesting that some kind of ritual object may have been held between the two hands.

The small bronze standing figure unearthed at the Jinsha site gives a sense of magic, whether in the form of the posture, the facial features, the crown and hat, the long braid at the back of the head, and the magic weapon at the waist. The shape of the bronze figure is the same as Sanxingdui's, showing the characteristics of Shu culture. In particular, the gesture of the hands is almost identical to that of the large bronze standing figure excavated from the pit No. 2 at Sanxingdui, as well as that of another small bronze figure with an animal-head shape, both of which are in a sacrificial pose. Though their shapes are different, they are the epitome of the shamans embodied with Shu features in sacrificial activities. Suppose the large, luxurious bronze figure at Sanxingdui embodies the king of Shu and the chief of shamans in great sacrificial activities. In that case, the small one excavated at the Jinsha site may symbolize the clan chiefs or clan shamans of Ancient Shu. Despite the different statuses and identities of the shamans they represent, the posture in the sacrificial activities is the same, vividly reflecting the prevalence of ritual activities and the flourishing of witchcraft in the Ancient Shu clan and Kingdom during the Shang and Zhou periods, and revealing the dominant status and important role of shamans who held both divine and royal power in Ancient Shu at that time.

In ancient times, there were many tribes and small states in southwest China. Sima Qian's famous book the *Records of the Grand Historian* has described the facts that: "There are more than tens of tribes with different rulers in the southwest Yi," "In the west part of southwest Yi, there are dozens of ethnic groups," and "To the north of Dian (today's Yunnan), there are also tens of emperors," "Some countrysides, towns and cities are settled together, and people cultivate their fields," "Some of the farmers pasture their animals so that they are without fixed quarters."

This is also recorded by Ban Gu in the *Book of Han*. Both books refer to the Han Dynasty, but dating back to the Shang and Zhou dynasties, the number of tribes, large or small, in the southwest part was probably much more. As Mr. Tong Enzheng said, the situation is closely related to the distinctive culture and geography of the southwest region, which lies between the two

*Bronze human
head from the
Sanxingdui site*

great rivers, the Yellow River and the Yangtze River, and the transition zone
between the Qinghai-Tibet Plateau and the middle and lower reaches of the
Yangtze, which has been a place of interaction and integration between the
livestock-raising peoples of the west and the agricultural peoples of the east
since ancient times. Therefore, the fragmentation of the Ancient Shu was
influenced by nature for a long time.

It is likely that the early Ancient Shu saw an evolution from a tribal
alliance to a chieftain society, leading to a co-ruler political situation. It seems
that the Ancient Shu Kingdom maintained a good order of co-rulership in
the Shang and Zhou dynasties; thus the Ancient Shu was prosperous in
social development and sacrificial activities. According to scholars, before
the destruction of Ba Shu by the Qin Dynasty (221–207 BC), there were at
least hundreds of small tribes in Ba Shu, the leaders of which were often
called "Rongbo," and Ba and Shu were also the chiefs of these Rongbo, as
well as the allied leaders of the tribal alliance. The numerous tribes and clans
of Ancient Shu shared different development conditions. While some clans
or tribes were joined in marriage and flourished, others may have declined
for various reasons, and the stronger clans or tribes may have replaced the
declining counterparts as the new co-owners, thus triggering the change of
dynasties in Ancient Shu. Thus, the Jinsha site, as an early habitat for the
clans of the Ancient Shu Kingdom, was under the political rule of the co-
rulers of Sanxingdui for a long time; the small bronze figures standing in
sacrificial activity provide good evidence.

FAR LEFT A bronze figure wearing a braided headband excavated at the Sanxingdui site

LEFT Bronze figure with youthful feminine beauty unearthed at the Sanxingdui site

This multi-clan alliance of the Ancient Shu Kingdom significantly differed from Central China and other regions in its social structure. The Yin-Shang Dynasty in the same period practiced a brutal mechanism of slavery. Archaeological findings in Yin Ruins told us that the slave-owning nobility of the Shang Dynasty frequently held rituals to heaven, ghosts and gods, and ancestors, which often killed people as sacrifices besides slaughtered cattle and sheep. Shang Dynasty also buried dogs, cattle, sheep, carriages, and slaves whose bodies were dismembered when palaces and temples were built. According to statistics, the number of immolated slaves is astonishing, about 1,000 immolated slaves were found in the tomb of the Shang Dynasty, and the horrifying facts were recorded on the unearthed oracle bones and history literature. In contrast, the Ancient Shu was less brutal under the co-ruler system, and no immolated slaves have been found in any of the Shang and Zhou period tombs excavated in Sichuan. Various sacrificial activities were frequently held in Ancient Shu; during the activity, the Shu people mainly used figure sculptures as the symbols of the ruling class and the shamans, without killing any people as sacrifices, making them seem more moderate. These facts showed that the Ancient Shu Kingdom was distinct from Central China in terms of its institutions, rituals, and sacrificial form and content.

Shamans held the central role of sacrificial activities in Ancient Shu; therefore, the bronze statues unearthed at the Sanxingdui and the Jinsha sites are invariably the symbol of shamans, mostly in sacrificial poses. What do these bronze statues want to show us? The moral is clearly revealed by the strange crown worn on the head of the small standing bronze figure excavated from the Jinsha site. The Sun and Immortal Birds Gold Ornament excavated at the Jinsha site has two portions with an inner part; one is a hollowed image and in the middle is a sun with 12 rays around it, which is very similar to the form of the strange crown worn on the head of the small bronze standing figure. Although the whirls of the crown of this bronze figure and the Sun and Immortal Birds Gold Ornament are 13 and 12 respectively, they are unusually similar in shape and composition, being equally spaced and resembling slightly curved ivory tusks, just like magical whirlpool giving a strong sense of dimension and reminding people of the dazzling light of the sun. If the shimmering disks and dazzling light of Sun and Immortal Birds Gold Ornament are a creative and magical expression of the Ancient Shu's worship of the sun, then the whirling, bizarre crown worn on the head of the bronze standing figure may have given a special meaning to the halo of the sun, and it is also a vivid reflection of the Ancient Shu's sun worship.

Numbers of archaeological studies tell us that sun worship was the dominant faith of the Ancient Shu people during the Shang and Zhou periods, occupying an important and prominent place in their frequent sacrificial activities. The large number of unearthed antiques in Sanxingdui have shown the facts, such as the sacred bronze tree, which is associated with the sun myth, and the large bronze standing figure with the figure of the sun on its crown, which clearly expresses the worship of the sun. The small standing bronze figure unearthed at the Jinsha site, wearing a crown symbolizing the sun's halo, undoubtedly expresses worship of the sun as well. All of these suggest that sun-oriented sacrificial activities were not only frequently held in the capital of the Sanxingdui Kingdom but were also important rituals performed by the Shu people in Jinsha. It is further speculated that this small standing bronze figure, a symbol of the leader or shaman of a clan or a tribe,

Bronze sacred tree from the
Sanxingdui site

ABOVE LEFT Small bronze standing figure from the tomb of Yu Country, Baoji, Shaanxi Province
ABOVE CENTER Bronze figure from the tomb of Yu Country, Baoji, Shaanxi Province
ABOVE RIGHT Small kneeling bronze figure holding a jade Zhang blade form the Sanxingdui site

may have acted as a herald of the sun during the sacrificial activity held by Ancient Shu, undertaking the role of a sun worshipper and praying for a good harvest year. In addition, it may have been seen as an emissary of the sun god, playing a role in communicating between man and god.

What the small bronze standing figure excavated from the Jinsha site holds is also a matter of debate. Scholars have speculated on the extremely exaggerated hands of the bronze figure excavated at Sanxingdui, with some suggesting that they are holding a jade cong or magical vessel, and others suggesting that they may be ivory. According to the fact, it is unlikely that the hands of the standing bronze figure are holding a jade cong with a square exterior and a round interior while holding a bent ivory or some kind of magic weapon is more plausible. Another bronze figure with a crowned animal head was excavated from the site of Sanxingdui, but what do the hands hold? The bronze figure is small, the ivory cannot be placed, and because the grip holes are clearly misaligned, some scholars believe that it may be holding two things or is simply a gesture. In addition, there are several bronze figures from the Sanxingdui site that hold Ya zhang or a vine symbolizing the Rui Zhi, an auspicious grass, which is also an important reference. Could the small bronze figure excavated at the Jinsha site hold in both hands the branches of Fusang or Ruomu (a sacred tree in Chinese myth) to welcome the sun? It is possible that it is some kind of auspicious symbol, ritual instrument, or object for sacrificing to the gods or communicating with the gods. It is

Bronze human head with gold mask excavated from the Sanxingdui site

worth mentioning the two bronze figures unearthed in the Rujiazhuang tombs No. 1 and No. 2 of the Yu Country burial complex in Baoji, Shaanxi; one bronze figure (male) has his hands raised over his right shoulder in an exaggerated circle, while the other (female) simply holds her hands out to the left and right as if in dancing, and the two hands shake in a huge round pattern, which is closely related to the Ancient Shu culture. The period of the two bronze figures is similar to that excavated in Jinsha, and there are similarities in shape and size, which can also be a reference. These excavated objects show that the bronze figures carved and cast by the Ancient Shu Kingdom or tribes during the Shang and Zhou period did have a variety of gestures in terms of the shape of their hands. Whatever the object held by the figure, or the gesture of the figure's hand-made, it is an expression of piety.

It is also interesting that the small bronze standing figure stands on the top of the insert, which is slightly square and separated at the upper end, much like an inverted Lei-shaped vessel from the early agrarian age. According to the excavators, a small amount of cinnabar remains on the crossbeam of the insert, which is a remnant of sacrificial activity, and some remaining traces of wood were found at the lower end of the insert; according to the facts, it is suggested that the small bronze standing figure was probably inserted for using on a wooden shrine or altar. Going forward, combining the bronze figure with wooden parts was probably a convention in Ancient Shu Kingdoms during the Shang and Zhou periods. For example, the numerous bronze human heads excavated at the site of Sanxingdui, with their pointed triangular shape under the neck, were probably mounted on the top of wooden bodies. It also suggests that the human-face figures excavated at the Sanxingdui site may have been mounted on wooden or clay bodies. These bronze heads and faces are of a lower status than the taller bronze standing figures and may represent the various clan tribes of the Ancient Shu Kingdom. Is that why they used a wooden body and a wooden base? As well as the reasons for the status relationship, it may also have had more to do with the fact that mine resources were limited in that time. The

small bronze standing figure excavated at the Jinsha site and the large bronze figure excavated at the Sanxingdui site are exactly the same according to the pose and shape, but there is a huge difference in size and in the complexity of the costume, as well as in the altar on which they stand, all of which form a stark contrast, showing the difference in status between the two. Obviously, the large standing bronze figure on the square bronze altar symbolizes the king of Shu and the head of the shamans, while other lower-status bronze figures are unqualified to be entitled to special treatment. This small standing bronze figure, as the symbol of the clan or tribe leaders and shamans of Jinsha, was cast in a smaller size and used only in conjunction with a wooden pedestal because of its status.

In summary, the small standing bronze figure excavated from the Jinsha site has profound connotations. Not only does it reveal a great deal of information about ritual activities and social life in Ancient Shu, but it also gives us a true account of the chronological and cultural connections between the Jinsha site and the ancient city of Sanxingdui in the Shang and Zhou period. When the bronze culture of Sanxingdui flourished, the ruler of the Jinsha site was probably only the head of a clan or tribe in the Ancient Shu Kingdom. Whether in the ancient city of Sanxingdui, the capital of the

Bronze standing figure from the Sanxingdui site

Ancient Shu Kingdom, or in the tribal settlement of the Jinsha site, various sacrificial activities such as sun worship and praying for a good harvest year were often held, although the content and the form were the same; but the former was grand and magnificent, while the latter was of a lower status and smaller scale. This difference in status and the size of the rituals is due to the relationship between them. It was only after Sanxingdui's destruction that the Jinsha tribe gradually flourished and replaced it. The small bronze figure tells us exactly what happened during the development of Jinsha from a tribal habitat to a kingdom's capital. As the archaeological excavations at the Jinsha site advanced and more material was published, we believe we will have an overall view of the site.

4

---◦◦◇◇◦◦---

The Charm of the Sun and Immortal Bird

The Sun and Immortal Birds Gold Ornament

In the first spring of the 21st century, an artifact unearthed at the Jinsha site became a radiant symbol of Chengdu. The Sun and Immortal Bird flying out of Chengdu will forever guard China's cultural heritage.

Many of the precious artifacts unearthed at the Jinsha site show extraordinary magical charm, the most typical of which is the Sun and Immortal Birds Gold Ornament. Today, when people drive past the magnificent overpass of the Chengdu Southern Extension Line, they will marvel at the image of the Sun and Immortal Birds In the first spring of the 21st century, an artifact was unearthed in an archaeological excavation, and it has become a shining symbol and the most beautiful scenery of Chengdu. On August 16th, 2005, the National Cultural Heritage Administration officially announced that the Sun and Immortal Birds Gold Ornament unearthed at the Jinsha site in Chengdu would be a symbol of China's cultural heritage. From then on, the immortal bird of the sun flying out of Chengdu will permanently guard China's cultural heritage.

The Sun and Immortal Birds Gold Ornament excavated from the Jinsha site is a pocket-sized artifact. It is round with an openwork pattern inside. The gold artifact is made of a thin gold leaf and weighs 20 g, measuring 12.5 cm in its outer diameter, 5.29 cm in its inner diameter, and 0.02 cm in thickness. The artifact is extraordinary in ingenuity and creativity, so it remains dazzling and exquisite thousands of years later. With the technique of hammering and cutting, the gold artifact is uniform in thickness, with neat and smooth edges. Its excellency in craftsmanship and ingenuity in design fully demonstrate the mature expertise of the craftsman. What is marvelous about the gold artifact is the pattern on it. It is like a symmetrical paper cut, which seems to be carefully cut by a mold. Both the overall layout and the subtleties of the pattern are meticulous, achieving extremely magical aesthetic appeal within a limited space. The openwork pattern on the artifact is divided into two layers: the inner and the outer. The center of the inner layer is a hollow circle, surrounded by 12 equidistant distributed ivory-shaped arc sharps, which are arranged in a pattern of clockwise rotating gears. The outer layer is four counterclockwise flying birds, which are symmetrically arranged, with the head of the former bird connected with the foot of the latter one. With necks and legs stretched out, the birds fly around the inner layer. The whole pattern is dynamic, as if it were a magical whirlpool, a rotating cloud, or a radiant sun in the sky, and people associate the four flying birds with the golden crows loading the sun and soaring through the sky. Archaeologists once put this wonderful artifact against a red background, and they found that its inner swirling pattern is like a rotating fireball, and the flying birds look like red firebirds. The immortal birds, which fly around the sun, are a vivid illustration of the myth of the sun in ancient times and have brought the rich association of the myth into full play.

Worship of the sun is probably one of the oldest topics in the march of mankind from barbarism to civilization. Because of its close relationship with nature and its vital role in the survival and reproduction of mankind, the sun

FAR LEFT Standing bird on the bronze sacred tree unearthed at the Sanxingdui site

LEFT Small bronze sacred tree unearthed at the Sanxingdui site

has been worshipped with reverence by the ancients since time immemorial, and interesting myths of the sun still circulate among the peoples of the world. Apollo was the well-known sun god in ancient Greek mythology, while the myth of the ten suns with its strong oriental character was widely spread in ancient China. They were widely spread in different ways in both the West and the East and had an important and far-reaching influence on the thoughts and behavior of ancient peoples, and history and culture as a whole. We know that the ancient Greeks and Romans shaped many statues of Apollo and built magnificent temples to Apollo. The figurative products of solar mythology in the West captured the attention of all Europeans. In the East, the myth of the ten suns is similar, from its mythological depictions to its sculptural and graphic forms, which are highly imaginative and awe-inspiring, and still sparkle with magic.

The *Classic of Mountains and Seas* and other ancient works contain many fantastic accounts of the mythical legends of the sun in ancient China. It is said that the ten suns were sons of Di Jun and Xi He. They had human and immortal characteristics and were also the incarnation of golden crows, three-legged, immortal birds of the sun. They bathed in the Tanggu and perched on the fusang trees. Every day, they took turns flying from the fusang tree, the immortal tree of the sun at the east pole, to the ruomu tree, the immortal tree of the sun at the west pole. In other words, every morning, the sun rose from the fusang tree and took the form of a golden crow or the immortal bird of the sun flying from east to west in the universe. At night, the sunset on the ruomu tree in the west. Such an amazing and magical scene reflects not only the ancient observation of sunrise and sunset but also the rich imagination of our ancestors about the immortal trees and birds. Archaeological evidence suggests that the myth of the ten suns was particularly prevalent in the Ancient Shu Kingdom in the upper reaches of the Yangtze during the Yin-Shang Dynasty, as evidenced by the bronze sacred tree unearthed at the Sanxingdui site. The bronze tree was divided into three tiers with a total of nine immortal birds perched on its branches, representing the scene of "nine suns on the lower branch," and the tree top was broken off when it was unearthed. Presumably, there should also be another immortal bird representing the scene of "one sun on the upper branch." It is a perfect portrayal of the myth of the ten suns. Significantly, the nine immortal birds perched on the sacred bronze tree all have eagle beaks and cuckoo bodies. The eagle is the most robust bird of prey soaring in the sky, while the cuckoo is the bird loved by our ancestors in Ancient Shu. The fusion of their features is probably the image of the golden crow in the sun, as the Ancient

Silk painting unearthed at the No. 1 Han tomb at Mawangdui, Changsha, Hunan Province

Shu people imagined. A human-faced bird statue was also unearthed at the Sanxingdui site, which was a wonderful representation of the unity of humans and immortal features, vividly portraying the personified sun god. In later ages, the myth of the ten suns spread more widely, as we can see on many Han Dynasty stone reliefs and brick reliefs unearthed throughout China. A painted picture of the golden crows and the sun is also found on a silk painting excavated from the Mawangdui Han tomb in Changsha, Hunan Province, which illustrates the circulation and influence of the myth of the Ten Days in later times. There is also a painting of a golden crow in the sun on the silk painting unearthed from the Mawangdui Han tomb in Changsha, Hunan Province. All these show the influence of the myth of the ten suns on later generations.

In the Ancient Shu period, when graphic language was the dominant form of language, sculpture and motifs were the primary means by which the skilled craftsmen presented the myth of ten suns and sun worship. The Ancient Shu, energetic and quick in mind, were particularly fond of reflecting their sophisticated spiritual world by means of imaginative images, which had probably been a long-standing tradition unique to the Ancient Shu since time immemorial. Their extraordinary strength is best demonstrated by the large number of artifacts unearthed at the Sanxingdui site. The Jinsha site, which is in line with the Sanxingdui site in terms of historical traditions and cultural connotations, has more creative ways to demonstrate this. The Sun and Immortal Birds Gold Ornament is a typical example. Its motif is so small and delicate, yet its symbolic meaning is so magnificent that it fully displays its magnificent and magical character from its form to its connotations.

Particularly noteworthy is that the Ancient Shu people of the Shang and Zhou periods not only worshipped the sun but also worshipped birds. Archaeological discoveries at the Sanxingdui site and the Jinsha site revealed that the Ancient Shu people took birds as totems, and the phoenix as well as immortal birds of the sun, had a special place in their spiritual world. Their concept of bird worship and totem was intertwined with sun worship and sun mythology, and they were usually extremely closely related.

Here again, the account of Di Jun is mentioned. In many myths and legends from ancient China, Di Jun and the Yellow Emperor were great gods of the East, with an exalted status similar to that of Zeus, the supreme deity of ancient Greek mythology. If the Yellow Emperor, as recorded in the ancient literature of the Central Plains, was the supreme ruler of heaven and earth in the minds of the ancient people of the Yellow River Basin, Di Jun, as recorded in some ancient texts such as the *Classic of Mountains and Seas*, was the heavenly emperor of the universe and the world in the southern Chinese cultural system. Di Jun not only had ten suns with Xi He but also had twelve moons with Chang Xi. Moreover, he had a kingdom of three-bodies with E Huang. He had also many other descendants, such as "Di Hong," "Black Tooth," "Ji Zhi," "Hou Ji,"

Bronze bird unearthed at the Jinsha site

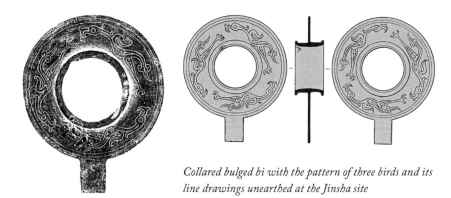

Collared bulged bi with the pattern of three birds and its line drawings unearthed at the Jinsha site

"Yu Huan," and "Yan Long" as mentioned in the *Classic of Mountains and Seas*. Di Jun's descendants revered immortal birds, and most of them had the ability to "drive four birds (four mythical creatures)." According to Mr. Yuan Ke, Di Jun is actually the incarnation of an immortal bird in the southern cultural system, so all of his descendants had an inseparable relationship with magical birds. From the mythological accounts which often recurred in the *Classic of Mountains and Seas*, the legend of "driving the four birds" reflected an imagination of driving and harnessing the immortal birds of the sun. Besides, the mettle and hope of the ancient people to overcome nature also seemed to be revealed. The fact that the four birds flying with the sun on the golden foil ornament are so strikingly consistent with the account of "driving the four birds" is not simply a coincidence but a vivid demonstration of the myth and legend with the faith of the ancient people.

The meaning of the Sun and Immortal Birds Gold Ornament at the Jinsha site is extremely rich. In the first sense, it takes the spinning fire wheel as a symbol of the radiant sun in the universe and the four flying birds as golden crows or immortal birds of the sun. The scene of golden crows soaring in the sky with the sun on their back gives a vivid representation of the Ancient Shu people's concept of bird worship and sun worship. In the second sense, the four birds on the gold ornament connote that Di Jun's descendants have the ability to "drive four birds," which are applied to show that both the maker and user are all descendants of Di Jun and they have a sacred kinship with the sun god. As descendants of Di Jun, they naturally enjoy noble status and have the undoubted power to rule and enslaving other tribes. In the third sense, the gold ornament probably shows the Ancient Shu's knowledge about the laws of nature; for example, the twelve rotating curved rays and the four flying birds represented twelve months, the Chinese zodiac, four seasons, four directions, etc. The sun in the middle may symbolize light, life, and eternity, and the four birds flying around the sun may also reflect the Ancient Shu's yearning for a better life, freedom, beauty, and unity. In short, the image is so distinctive and full of strong emotions. In the Ancient Shu Kingdom, although the ruler of the Jinsha site was only a tribal leader and clan wizard, the Sun and Immortal Birds Gold Ornament showed his extraordinary ambition and aspirations. The historical development of the Ancient Shu succeeded in proving that this tribe was by no means an ordinary people.

It is easy to associate the Sun and Immortal Birds Gold Ornament with the bronze bi disk excavated at the same time at the Jinsha site, whose wonderful pattern and rich symbolism are well worth exploring and appreciating. The bronze bi disk with a short handle is round with a round hole in the center. There is a raised high collar around the hole. The disk measures 10.24–10.36 cm in its outer diameter, 4.03–4.31 cm in its inner diameter, 2.9 cm in the height of the collar, 2.67 cm in the width of the side wheel, 2.26 cm in the length of the short handle, and weighs 280 g. Both sides of its side wheel are engraved with the same flying bird pattern, that is, three immortal birds with their heads and tails connected. Outside the bird pattern, there are two circles as the sidebar. All the images are carved simply and smoothly in shaded lines. The three immortal birds are also in the shape of flying birds, with their necks forward and legs extended backward. In addition, the birds' hooked beaks, round eyes, gorgeous long crowns, and flowing tails are meticulously depicted, making them vivid and animated. Compared with the Sun and Immortal Birds Gold Ornament, the bronze bi disk is similar not only in size but also in the symbolic meaning expressed by the image decoration. Isn't the round hole with a raised collar around a symbol of a sun? Don't the three immortal birds show the same scene of flying from east to west in the sky with the sun on their back? Both the exaggerated presentation and the rich imagery give a sense of magic. The bronze bi disk was likely a product of the sun myth and the sun worship that flourished in the Ancient Shu period, and it might also be an influential artifact in ritual activities with sun worship as its theme.

From the perspective of appreciation, the originality and expressiveness of these two artifacts, as well as the romantic emotions and unrestrained

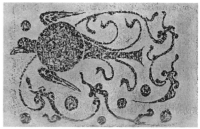

ABOVE LEFT The picture of "Golden Crow in the Sun" on a Han Dynasty portrait brick unearthed in Xindu, Sichuan Province

ABOVE RIGHT The picture of "Golden Crow Flying Along with the Sun" on a Han Dynasty portrait stone unearthed in Nanyang, Henan Province

LEFT The picture of "Three-legged Crow" on a Han Dynasty portrait stone unearthed in Tanghe County, Henan Province

spirit presented in their images, are really amazing. There are also some subtle differences between them, such as the immortal birds flying with the sun on their back. As far as we know, there are four birds on the Sun and Immortal Birds Gold Ornament, while there are three on the bronze bi disk. Are there also subtle differences in their symbolic meaning? In the *Classic of Mountains and Seas*, there are accounts of three green birds and colorful birds, stating that "there are three green birds with red heads and black eyes, one of them named Dali, another is Shaoli, and the third is the green bird." In addition, "there are three colorful birds, which are immortal birds like the phoenix, one of them is a Huangniao bird (the female phoenix), another is a Luanniao bird (the same species of phoenix), and the third is a Fengniao bird (the male phoenix)." All these birds are closely related to the Queen Mother of the West (Xiwangmu). Are the three immortal birds carved on the bronze bi disk unearthed from the Jinsha site, with their gorgeous crowns and tails and the athletic flying figure related to the above myths and legends? According to the legend, there were three green birds that fetched food for the Queen Mother of the West. Some scholars believe that these birds are written as Sanzuwu in both the version of the Song Dynasty's (AD 960–1279) *Classic of Mountains and Seas* and Sima Xiangru's *Da Ren Fu* in *Historical Records*, while according to "*Huainanzi · the Quintessential Spirit*," the Sanzuwu were called "Cunwu in the sun," also known as "Yangwu" or "Jinwu," which were considered to be the essence of the sun. Actually, they were all immortal birds of the sun. The Sanzuwu were often depicted in Han Dynasty portraits as golden crows flying in a round sun, or as strange crows with three legs standing in a sun, which is obviously a misinterpretation made by the Han Dynasty people thus making a false portrayal of the myths. In fact, there are other ways to represent them since the Shang and Zhou dynasties, such as three birds around the sun on some bronze mirrors in the Warring States period and the Qin Dynasty, which often depicted Sanzuwu as three sacred birds flying around the sun, all three with one foot, a depiction that is probably closer to the original image in the myths. The three immortal birds depicted on the bronze bi disk unearthed at the Jinsha site are also typical with long necks, a single leg, gorgeous feathers, and wings, and flying around the sun. It is obvious that the depiction is exactly the Sanzuwu in the myths and legends, and it is one of the most classical representations of the mythical meaning.

The bronze bi disk excavated from the Jinsha site reveals the Ancient Shu people's beliefs of bird worship and sun worship, as does the Sun and Immortal Birds Gold Ornament. Documentary records and excavated materials show that bird worship and sun worship were not only the theme of the Ancient Shu people's spiritual world but also the common beliefs of all tribes at that time. In the history of the Ancient Shu, such dynasties as Baiguan, Yufu, and Duyu, as well as other tribes in Ancient Shu society at that time, all worshipped the immortal birds and the sun. The Kaiming Dynasty was no exception, with a special reverence for the sun and the immortal birds. In terms of their use, it is likely that both of the precious artifacts were used by the Ancient Shu people in their grand sacrifice activities, or they might be offerings in the ancestral temples or shrines of the ruling class at the Jinsha site. The wonderful patterns on the Sun and Immortal Birds Gold Ornament and the bronze bi disk can be rated as masterpieces of the immortal bird. They represented not only the highest reverence of the Ancient Shu era but also the sacred symbols in the minds of the Ancient Shu people.

5

—◦◦◇◦◦—

Interpretation of the Symbolic Meaning of the Frog-Like Gold Foil

The frog in the frog-like gold foil is not an ordinary frog in nature but a divine frog created by the skilled craftsmen of the Ancient Shu tribe through ingenuity and imagination.

The Ancient Shu people mined and used gold from an early age. Their processing of gold reached a very high level in the Shang and Zhou periods, as revealed in the gold scepter, gold mask, tiger-shaped gold foil, large fish-shaped gold foil, and other gold artifacts excavated from the Sanxingdui site. Dozens of gold ornamental objects unearthed from the Jinsha site, such as the gold mask, gold crown band, the Sun and Immortal Birds Gold Ornament, frog-like gold foil, trumpet-shape gold object, case-shape gold object are also a refreshing change of pace with bizarre patterns and a quirky style. We have already appreciated the magnificent ornament of the Sun and Immortal Birds; now let's move on to the frog-like gold foil, which is rich in symbolic meaning.

Two frog-like gold foils were excavated from the Jinsha site, both of which had essentially the same shape, size, and production techniques, one more complete, and one with a slightly mutilated head. The first is 6.96 cm long, 6 cm wide, and 0.004–0.16 cm thick. The other is 6.94 cm long, 6.17 cm

Frog-like gold foil and its line drawing excavated from the Jinsha site

Frog carving on a bronze drum unearthed in Jiangchuan, Yunnan Province

wide, and 0.012–0.1 cm thick. Judging from the dimensions, it can be seen that they are all made of very thin gold foils. The production process shows that hammering, stamping, and cutting techniques were used, and the same mold may have been used. In the detailed decoration, burin engraving was used. Although the outer edges of the frog-like gold foil are cut roughly, resulting in uneven edges, considerable care is taken in the presentation of the form and ornamentation. For example, the curled limbs, the gourd-shaped head, the pointed peach-shaped beak, juxtaposed pairs of rounded eyes, the protrusions on both sides of the abdomen, the pointed end of the tail, and the string patterns and bead-like teat patterns extending along both sides of the backbone to the limbs are all distinctive. In particular, the continuous arrangement of rounded and highly convex teat patterns represents spots and bumps on the body of a frog or toad, adding a sense of vividness to the form. The limbs of the frog-like gold foil are symmetrically twisted, which are very peculiar and even a little treacherous, showing that the craftsmen of the time were also original in their treatment of limbs. The frog-like gold foil is an abstract, deformed animal, and judging from the overall shape and detailed features, it is most likely to be a frog or toad.

Since ancient times, frogs and toads have been auspicious objects for some ethnic groups in southwest China. At the site of Sanxingdui, stone toads were excavated in the form of crawling with their mouths open and teeth exposed, and their bodies covered in bumps, which appear to be vivid and realistic. The stone toads are similar to the frog-like gold foil excavated at the Jinsha site. On the bronze drums of the Han Dynasty unearthed in Yunnan, Guangxi, and other places, frogs or toads were cast around the surface. From a large amount of material data provided by archaeological discoveries, there were frog patterns on painted pottery as early as the Yangshao Culture (a Neolithic culture widespread in China in the central Yellow River) period. For example, on the Majiayao-type pottery, there are both realistic and abstract depictions of frogs jumping. On the early painted pottery of the Banpo type, there are also vivid frog jumping postures depicted in a simple manner. From the distribution range, a large number of frog motifs have been unearthed from the famous Yangshao Village in Mianchi County, Henan Province, and Miaodigou in Shaanxi County, Henan Province (now Shaanzhou District, Sanmenxia City), through Xiguan Fort in Huayin County (now Huayang City) and Jiangzhai in Lintong County (now Lintong District, Xi'an City), Shaanxi Province, to Majiayao in Gansu Province, and Liuwan in Ledu County, Qinghai Province. The frog motifs in these pottery patterns are both figurative, freehand, and abstract. The rich and colorful patterns and gorgeous and harmonious colors are rare in the world. Especially the frog motifs on the pottery excavated at Liuwan, Qinghai, can be arranged in a complete sequence, which is breathtaking. Some scholars, after thorough research, have concluded that these frog motifs probably reflect the fertility cult of the ancestors and are also related to the origin of the moon myth. For example, the fish and frog motifs excavated at Jiangzhai, Lintong County, Shaanxi Province, present the custom of holding a "Fish and Frog Festival" at that time to pray for fertility and prosperity. The Majiayao-type pottery basin with dance motifs excavated at Shang Sunjiazhai, Datong County, Qinghai Province, also has a vivid depiction of this.

There are also many records about frogs and toads in classic Chinese literature, such as the *Huainanzi · the Quintessential Spirit*, which writes that "there is Cunwu in the sun and a toad in the moon. If the sun and the moon do not follow their normal course, they will be eroded and lose their brilliance." While in the *Huainanzi · A Forest of Persuasions*, there is also a saying that "the moon shines on the world and is eclipsed by the Zhanzhu. Zhanzhu is also known as the toad. Therefore, the saying means the lunar eclipse is due to the moon being eroded by a toad. In addition, the silk painting, unearthed from Mawangdui No. 1 Han tomb in Changsha, Hunan Province, depicts a toad standing on the crescent moon with a mouth-spitting cloud. On some Han Dynasty murals and Han Dynasty portrait stones or portrait bricks unearthed around China, there are also similar

The image of "Fish and Frog Festival" on a painted pottery pot excavated in Shangsunjiazhai, Datong County, Qinghai Province

The motif of fish and frog on a painted pottery basin of Yangshao Culture excavated from the Jiangzhai site in Lintong, Shaanxi Province

LEFT *The picture of "Changxi Holding the Moon" on a Han Dynasty portrait stone unearthed in Nanyang, Henan Province*

images. We can see from this that in ancient times, there was a widespread sun myth and a moon myth. If Cunwu (that is, Sanzuwu, also known as, "golden crows" or "Yang crows") are the immortal birds of the sun that carry the sun in flight, then the toad is symbol of the moon god according to the ancients. There is not only the myth and legend of the ten suns in the *Classic of Mountains and Seas* but also the record that "Chang Xi, Di Jun's wife, gave birth to twelve moons, and began to bathe the moons." In *Master Lü's Spring and Autumn Annals · Wugong*, there is also a saying that "Xihe observes the movement of the sun and Shangyi observes the movement of the moon as the basis for formulating the calendar." Some scholars believe that the myth of the goddess Chang'e flying to the moon evolved from this. Qu Yuan's *Chu Ci · Tianwen* says that "What virtue does the moon have that it can die and be reborn? What is the black spot in the middle of the moon? Is it hidden in the rabbit's belly?" Through the information revealed by these handed-down records, it is clear that the origin of moon myths and legends is quite ancient and widespread, with Chang Xi being the moon mother or moon god personified in the minds of the ancients, and the toad being regarded as a symbol of the moon. Ancient ancestors often used their imagination when

LEFT *Frog spear excavated in Jinning, Yunnan Province*

ABOVE *Stone toad excavated from the Sanxingdui site*

observing celestial events and associated them with animals. For example, the ancients might have thought that there was a Sanzuwu in the sun when they noticed that the sun has sunspots. Seeing the shadow of the moon, they said that there were toads in the moon. It naturally related to the limitations of the ancient people's understanding of the universe and the world.

It is worth asking why the ancients linked the moon with the toad. This is indeed a very interesting question. Some scholars believe that there may be two reasons: one is observation and association. Because the moon can only be seen at night, toads are also nocturnal animals, and there are dark shadows in the moon resembling toads, so it is easy to be linked to myths and legends. The other is reverence. In ancient times, it is likely that the toad was a totemic symbol worshipped by some clans or tribes, and because of observation and association, they believed that their totem ancestors were not ordinary animals, but divine toads or divine frogs from the moon, so the two were compared, thus forming the custom of worship and sacrifice. As some scholars say, primitive people, and even people in a certain dynasty, often believed that their ancestors were dual in nature, being both mortal flesh and descended from the gods. The most common was the belief that the clan or tribe is the descendant of the sun, or the sun god and the moon god. Worship of the sun god and the moon god, as well as the myths and legends derived from it, were obviously inseparable from the thinking mode of the ancestors.

The worship of toads and frogs by the ancients is probably due to multiple reasons. In the early days of primitive society, frogs, like fish, were probably one of the foods of the ancestors. Because of their prolific fertility and the similarity between the belly of a frog and that of a pregnant woman, which is round and enlarged, the frog became a symbol of female fertility in many primitive tribes and clans. And because the cry of frogs is similar to the cry of babies, some ancient clans worship frogs as totems. As reproduction and totemic symbols were of paramount importance to primitive peoples, it is not surprising that the frog was regarded as a sacred animal and given special symbolic meaning in the social life of matrilineal clans. According to some scholars, it is likely that the mythology of Nuwa is also closely related to the ancient ancestors' worship of frogs, suggesting that Nuwa may have been an ancient tribal leader who viewed frogs as totems, and being deified as a frog god and creator god in later generations.

Toads and frogs were valued by ancestors in ancient times, which had a lot to do with the living environment and agricultural production. The ancients discovered early on that frogs could predict weather changes, such as whether a thunderstorm was coming or whether there was a big drought by changes in the sound of the frog's song, which triggered the imagination of primitive people, who believed that frogs were mysterious. Our primitive ancestors, especially those who had just entered the farming era, discovered through long-term observation that frogs not only had a powerful ability to reproduce and breed but could also respond quickly and accurately to different weather changes; thus a sense of awe was created in their hearts for this unknowable power, which naturally led to the concept of frog worship. It is worth noting that the worship of frogs in ancient times was often highly practical and evolved into a custom of taking frogs to pray for rain. This ritual practice was prevalent in ancient times and popular in the Yellow River Basin, the Yangtze River Basin, and vast areas in the south, especially among the ancient tribes in the south, and it survived until the Han Dynasty. In Dong Zhongshu's *Luxuriant Dew of the Spring and Autumn Annals*, Volume 16, he gave a detailed account of the ritual activities of fetching toads for rain during the dry season in various parts of China. The rock paintings of Youjiang, Guangxi Province, depicted a number of figures standing and jumping like frogs, representing the dance of the Zhuang ancestors in a ritual for rain. According to folklore passed down in the Zhuang region, the frog

The golden crow in the sun and the toad in the full moon on a Han Dynasty portrait stone unearthed in Nanyang, Henan Province

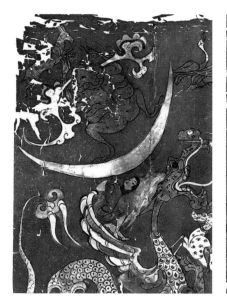 

The toad on the curved moon and the golden crow in the sun on the silk painting excavated in the Mawangdui No. 1 Han tomb in Changsha, Hunan Province

was believed to be the son of the King of Thunder, and also the messenger sent to earth by the King of Thunder. When people on the earth needed rain, the frog would make a noise, and the King of Thunder would make it rain. Later, the folk custom of worshipping frogs was formed, and the activity of worshipping the frog god was held grandly in the first month of every year, called the "Frog Festival" (commonly known as the "Maguai Festival"). It is still a major traditional festival in the Zhuang settlement in the upper reaches of the Hongshui River in Guangxi. In some other minority areas in the south of China, the ancient custom of frog sacrifice can also be seen. Even in Pu Songling's *Strange Tales of a Lonely Studio: Singing Frogs*, it is written that "people in the Yangtze River and the Hanshui River believe in the frog god" and there is a witchcraft activity of the "frog god race."

The fact that the pre-Qin custom of sacrificing frogs for rain was still prevalent in the Han Dynasty and later generations is a testament to its influence. If it had not been an important ritual in ancient times, it would not have had such a widespread and far-reaching impact. We can therefore assume that "sacrificing frogs for rain" was probably also an important ritual in Ancient Shu during the Shang and Zhou periods. In the Sanxingdui period, there were stone toads, and the Jinsha site had elaborately crafted frog-like gold foil, which demonstrates the Ancient Shu's reverence for frogs or toads and may be remnants of frog rituals in the Ancient Shu. According to the archaeological findings of the Sanxingdui and Jinsha sites, rituals in Ancient Shu were exceptionally prosperous, not only diverse in form but also with characteristics of witchcraft. Among rituals frequently held in Ancient Shu, moon worship and "sacrificing frogs for rain" were probably very important, in addition to sun worship which we are familiar with. The information revealed by ancient documents and environmental archaeology shows that the Shang and Zhou periods in China were a period of climate variability, with not only floods but also severe droughts. The Ancient Shu Kingdom, located in the inland basin of the upper reaches of the Yangtze River, was no exception, and floods and droughts were also frequent. In addition to the great floods at the time of Duyu and Bieling, there were also several major droughts and probably even a severe one similar to that in the Central Plains at the time of Cheng Tang (founding monarchs of the Shang Dynasty). Therefore, the ritual of "sacrificing frogs for rain" was probably very important at that time. From this, it is clear that the frog-like gold foil excavated from the Jinsha site and the stone toads from the Sanxingdui site were both used in the frog sacrifice rituals that were prevalent at the time, both as symbols of sacrifice and as offerings for rain. In contrast, the dazzling frog-like gold foil seemed to represent the devotion of the sacrificer better than the round stone toads. At the same time, it also expressed the urgency of praying for rain. The fact that the rulers of the Jinsha site also made numerous stone kneeling figures to "insolate witches and the disabled under the sun for rain" suggested that there was indeed a continuous drought in Shu at the time. The drought was so severe that the rulers went to great lengths to use precious gold to make golden frogs for sacrifice in the hope that the frog god would be moved to relieve the drought as soon as possible and bless a good agricultural harvest. These rituals showed a more obvious witchcraft overtone, which was in keeping with the widespread witchcraft of the Ancient Shu period.

The symbolic meaning of the frog-like gold foil is quite rich. In addition to its ritual use for praying for rain, its shape may also be the image of the toad or the frog god on the moon in the minds of the Ancient Shu people, which should have some relationship with the myth and legend of the moon that was widely spread in ancient times. The realistic and abstract style of the frog-like gold foils, as well as their mystery, fully illustrate that they are not ordinary frogs in nature, but divine frogs created by the skilled craftsmen of the Ancient Shu tribe through ingenuity and imagination. Although sun worship was always dominant at both the Sanxingdui and Jinsha sites, the stone toads and frog-like gold foil suggest that the Ancient Shu also practiced moon worship, and the two are fully comparable in the magnificence of their myths and legends. Second, we cannot ignore the fertility worship revealed by the frog-like gold foil. For the Ancient Shu Kingdom during the Shang and Zhou periods, the development of agriculture and population reproduction must have been a major priority for each clan or tribe. Moreover, taking the frog as a symbol of fertility worship was common in ancient times, and the strong desire to have a good harvest and a strong tribe was no exception for all ancient tribes. Therefore, the Ancient Shu were likely to practice a special form of frog ritual as a form of fertility worship, and the elaborate frog-like gold foil made by the Ancient Shu may contain this kind of connotation. Furthermore, it is possible that the frog-like gold foil was an auspicious object loved and revered by the Ancient Shu people and may even be a totemic symbol of a clan or a tribe. Totem, as a relic of ancient times, still had significant continuity and distinct performance in the social life of the Ancient Shu Kingdom during the Shang and Zhou periods. It is not due to the backwardness of Ancient Shu, but is inseparable from a large number of Ancient Shu tribes, the unique social structure of the Ancient Shu state, the inclusive reverence of the Ancient Shu people, the flourishing witchcraft and frequent rituals of the Ancient Shu era, and the special geographical environment of the inland basin in the upper reaches of the Yangtze River. It is because of these factors that the distinctive and unique Ancient Shu culture was formed. In a sense, it can be said that the frog-like gold foils excavated from the Jinsha site are vivid reflections of reverence for ancient customs with characteristics of Ancient Shu culture in the Shang and Zhou dynasties.

In summary, the frog-like gold foil excavated at the Jinsha site is indeed rich in connotations. In terms of cultural connotation, it is a symbol of reverence in the minds of the Ancient Shu, as is the Sun and Immortal Birds Gold Ornament. In terms of application, it is likely that they were precious offerings in the clan temples or shrines of the rulers in the Jinsha site, or important sacrifices. All in all, the frog-like gold foils are indeed wonderful creation of the Ancient Shu. The rich connotations and artistic charm they display provide us with new materials and reveal new content for our understanding of the myths, legends, and ritual activities of the Ancient Shu during the Shang and Zhou periods. Their importance in exploring the history and culture of Ancient Shu, as well as their significance in the field of art, archaeology, and other academic research, can be self-evident.

6

———◦◦◇◦◦———

Mysteries about Gold Crown Band

With exquisite shapes and imaginative patterns, the gold artifacts unearthed at the Jinsha site embody the Ancient Shu people's concept of reverence, clan consciousness, social customs, and aesthetic tastes.

Though the gold artifacts unearthed at the Jinsha site and Sanxingdui site are different in feature and style, they display consistency in their cultural heritage. With exquisite shapes and imaginative patterns, these artifacts tell the history of gold mining and the processing skills of the Ancient Shu people. More importantly, they embody the Ancient Shu people's concept of reverence, social customs, clan consciousness, aesthetic tastes, and many mysterious stories that make for rich associations.

Among the gold artifacts unearthed at the Jinsha site, the amazing gold crown band is of great significance in the history of archaeology. The band, in the shape of a circle, is relatively narrow in width and slightly wider at the top and narrower at the bottom. When unearthed, it was broken into a long strip. Later, it was restored and well-reserved at the Jinsha Site Museum. The band weighs 44 g, measuring 19.6 to 19.9 cm in diameter, 2.68 to 2.8 m in width, and 0.02 cm in thickness. Like other gold artifacts, the gold crown band was made through the process of hampering and folding, and on its surface, vivid and exquisite patterns were carved. Considering its texture, shape, size, and function, the band obviously could not serve as a waistband,

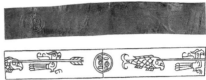

The gold crown band unearthed from the Jinsha site

Part of the gold crown band from the Jinsha site and its line drawing

Gold crown band from the Jinsha site and its line drawing

for its diameter is less than 20 cm after it is folded. Therefore, Yu Weichao, an archaeologist, made a reasonable speculation that the band functioned as a crown band worn on the head. The band might either be a decoration on the luxurious crown of the rulers, or an object used on occasion of grand sacrifices by heads or wizards of the Ancient Shu.

The most astonishing part of the gold crown band is the composite pattern on its surface, which is so skillfully carved that even the subtleties are clearly visible. The overall pattern is composed of four parts, with a symmetrical layout. The central part of the pattern is a fantastic round sun image, flanked by a fish, a bird and an arrow. Each part of the pattern is linked by the image of a round sun. In this way, the patterns are smooth in lines and rich in connotations. The birds are all depicted with strong necks, hooked beaks, long tails, and bright eyes. With claws and legs stretching forward and wings rising, the birds are lifelike. The fish are relatively fat, with large heads, round eyes, slightly hooked mouths, and rising beards. The scales on the fish, the long and short fins on the back and abdomen, and the curly tail are depicted very vividly. In general, the birds are more abstract and exaggerated, while the fish are more realistic. Most striking is the long shaft feathered arrows, shot from the round sun in the center to the heads of the birds and the fish on either side, across the neck of the bird and into the body of the fish. The images of the round suns are also of great interest. Each of them is composed of an outer circle and an inner circle in which there are two smaller symmetrical circles with two horizontal lines at each side,

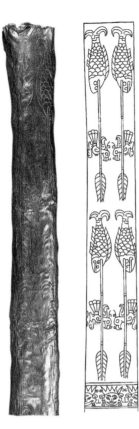

Gold scepter unearthed at the Sanxingdui site

symbolizing both the round sun and a human or animal face. In the overall layout of the gold crown band pattern, one of the sun images is located right in the center of the front, in a central position. It seems to tell us that the sun is dominant throughout the scene, and it is from here that the powerful long shafts of feathered arrows are shot at the fish and birds on either side, thus indicating its domination over the fate of the birds and fish. Does this suggest that the round sun with rich connotations is a manifestation of the Ancient Shu people's worship of the sun and a symbol of the Ancient Shu ruler's divine power and royal power? Maybe the birds and fish shot by the feathered arrow are a true portrayal of the fishing and hunting life in the Ancient Shu era, or the fish-bird totem worshipped by some clans or tribes in the Ancient Shu ethnic group? In short, there are rich symbolic meanings behind the patterns. One will be amazed at the creative designs in all their splendor and brilliance and marvel at the magical connotations and the bold vitality when looking closely at these exaggerated yet realistic images.

The patterns on the gold crown band, as a precious relic of the Ancient Shu people, manifest not only the creator's rich imagination but also his knowledge regarding the Ancient Shu Kingdom. As their connotation is far more complicated and magical than what we can imagine, it is interesting to explore and interpret these delightful images further. The band reminds us of the gold scepter unearthed at the pit No. 1 of Sanxingdui. Patterns on the scepter are similar to those on the band. Although their design and presentation are just the same, there are differences. First, the patterns are arranged in different directions because of their different uses. The gold crown band serves as a decoration of the crown worn on the head while the gold scepter is held in the hand. Hence the patterns on the band are horizontally arranged while those on the scepter, vertically. Second, they are

different in layout, which is determined by their unique shape. The patterns on the band, with a limited width, are arranged symmetrically in one row. In this way, the decoration offers a better visual effect and highlights the images in the front. Unlike the band, the gold skin of the scepter is wider when unfolded so that the patterns are arranged in two rows. In this way, when the wooden core is rolled to make a gold scepter, the double rows of patterns can fill its round body, giving a sense of continuity. With different ways to highlight things that the Ancient Shu people worshipped, those patterns also show the artist's creative design and exquisite craftsmanship. It is noteworthy that below the main pattern of the scepter are two human figures which are arranged symmetrically in front and back. They wear triangle-like long earrings and a crown in the shape of a petal or serration. With curving eyebrows above big eyes, animal ears, a wide mouth, and a round face, the two figures show a cheerful smile. They are also depicted with double hooks, which separate them from the main pattern, and some scholars believe that they may be a portrayal of the sun god. Likewise, on the gold crown band are four identical double-circle patterns which symbolize the sun but look like a human face or an animal face. Although the patterns on the two artifacts are different in arrangement, they have a similarity in their cultural meaning and symbolic significance. The patterns on the scepter are more realistic, while those on the band look abstract.

The picture of "Houyi Shooting Nine Suns" on the picture stone excavated in Nanyang, Henan Province (Han Dynasty)

Despite their uniqueness in artistic representation, the patterns on both the gold crown band and the gold scepter share the same cultural and symbolic meanings. They are all vivid "image language of Bashu," and it is likely that they are all given the same symbolism by the makers and users.

What exactly do the patterns on the gold scepter and the gold crown band tell us? As the written language emerged late, while image language was much more popular in the Ancient Shu Kingdom, people at that time preferred to express what they worshipped and recorded what happened in history with patterns. The Shu people were imaginative and adept at conveying rich connotations with simple pictures, which was reflected in their art of modeling and ornamentation. According to ancient documents, in the history of Ancient Shu, there were clans such as the Chancong, Baiguan, Yufu, Duyu, Kaiming, etc. The rise and decline of these tribes constituted the history of the Shu Kingdom. For more than half a century, important archaeological discoveries in the Chengdu Plain have revealed a large number of Ancient Shu remains, proving that the bewildering legends of the Ancient Shu are not false. Therefore, some scholars believe that the scepter unearthed in pit No. 1 in Sanxingdui is probably related to the legendary era of Yu Fu, the king of Shu. According to *Biography of Kings in Shu Kingdom* and other accounts, Yufu was both a mythological figure and the name of a clan, which had already declined by the time of the reign of Du Yu, the Emperor of Wang. If the scepter was a symbol of either the power of the ruler of the Ancient Shu Kingdom or an object used in sacrifices, would the picture of the arrow shot in the head of the fish through the bird's neck indicate the demise of the Tribe of Yufu? Does the fish on the band also represent the fall of Yufu tribe if it could be linked to the patterns on the gold crown band? Given that the gold crown band and the gold scepter were made in different times, the above speculation is rather far-fetched. It is more reasonable to take the patterns as symbols of the Shu People's sense of worship and mutual relationship, rather than a reflection of the rise and fall of dynasties. Based on the illustrations above, the following part will analyze the meanings of the patterns from three aspects.

First, both the sun god in the shape of the human face on the gold scepter and the round sun on the gold crown band express a strong sense of sun reverence, indicating that the bearer of the scepter and the wearer of the crown band were both descendants of Di Jun and had a close relationship with the sun god. The sun worship embodied in the two artifacts is similar to what is manifested in the Sun and Immortal Birds Gold Ornament at the Jinsha site and the bronze sacred tree in the second pit of the Sanxingdui site. Likewise, some round copper pendants excavated at Sanxingdui are also engraved with a round sun, which is very similar to that on the gold crown band of the Jinsha site. From what is mentioned above, it can be concluded

FROM LEFT TO RIGHT Bronze bird with phoenix head from the Sanxingdui site
Bronze phoenix from the Sanxingdui site
Bronze bird from the Sanxingdui site
Phoenix-head bronze bell from the Sanxingdui site

that sun worship is one of the Ancient Shu people's traditions and played a critical role in their life.

Second, the patterns also reflect the Shu people's sense of community and their worship of birds. Ancient classics like the *Classic of Mountains and Rivers* writes that most descendants of Diqun were able to "drive four animals." Thus, the four birds on the band and scepter may be a manifestation of the legend. Meanwhile, the birds and fish also indicate that some of the tribes in the Ancient Shu Kingdom worshipped the two kinds of living beings and perhaps some regarded the fish and bird as their totems. The Shu Kingdoms, including Yufu, Duyu and Kaiming had a tradition of worshipping fish and birds.

Third, the patterns show a kind of kingly momentum of holding the divine power and governing all ethnic groups, which is permeated with unrestrained heroic feelings. The arrows are reminiscent of the myth "Houyi Shoots the Sun." It is recorded in ancient classics, including *Zhuangzi · On Leveling All Things*, Liu An's of the Western Han Dynasty the *Huainanzi · Ben Jing Xun*, and Wang Chong's of the Eastern Han Dynasty (AD 25–220) *Discourses on Hengs · Sensational Void*. It is said that in ancient times, there were ten suns which resulted in a severe drought, scorching all plants. It was not until Houyi shot nine of them with feathered arrows that everything returned to normal. Thus, the arrows on the band and the scepter are likely to symbolize this story. More importantly, the patterns represent a dauntless heroic spirit.

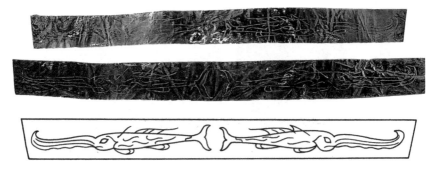

Gold belt with fish pattern and its line drawing

In addition to the gold band and the gold scepter, two gold bands which are fish with the head of a bird were also excavated at the Jinsha site. One of them measures 21.1–21.6 cm in length, 2.01–2.03 cm in width, and 0.02 cm in height. The other weighs 11 g, with a height and width the same as the first one, measuring 21.1–21.85 cm in length. Both of them are in the shape of an inverted trapezium. Similar to the gold crown band in processing, they are made from gold foils and carved with exquisite patterns. As for function, judging from their shapes, they might serve as decorations on crowns or ornaments for wearing. Provided that the gold crown band was exclusive to the rulers of Ancient Shu Kingdom, the owners of the two bands might be significant figures only inferior to the rulers. This can be seen from the differences between patterns on the artifacts. Compared with patterns on the gold crown band, those on the bands are less complicated. Consequently, the patterns lack the idea of sun worship and kingliness and are likely to show a fantastic totemic veneration and a strong sense of clan affiliation.

Let's take a look at the patterns on the bands. Both of them are carved with a pair of peculiar fish with their tails facing each other and their heads pointing outwards. The fish are quite strange. Their front parts are birds' heads with exaggerated beaks. Their bodies are long, like mallets, with fins on their backs and abdomens. Their bodies are not carved with scales but have several water ripples to indicate that they are swimming fast. What's more, they have exaggerated long beaks, which resembles birds' beaks, but are different from the common beak. The front of the long beak is upturned and slightly hooked backward, and the lower edges of the beaks have a wavy curve reminiscent of the beak of a pelican or other bird. Unlike the eyes of

Vertical-eyed bronze mask from the Sanxingdui site

fish or bird, their eyes, in the shape of an olive, are similar to those of humans or animals. In short, no counterpart of the fish can be found in the real world. They are special and incredible.

The unique image composed of fish and birds are bound to be endowed with special meanings. There are also other composite bronze artifacts unearthed at the Sanxingdui site, such as the bronze bird with a human face, and a bronze vertical-eyed figure that combines human and animal features.

Additionally, similar patterns are also found in in the *Classic of Mountains and Seas: Under the Seas*. For example, there are animals with human faces, creatures with tigers' heads and the claws of birds, and Zhu Rong (god of fire in ancient Chinese legends) with an animal's body and a human's face, riding two dragons, etc. This indicates that it was a popular custom for the Ancient Shu people to design composite patterns as their tribes' symbols. Thus, the patterns of the two gold bands mentioned above are perhaps a reflection of their customs.

The fish and the bird were probably the two most important clan symbols among the Ancient Shu. The fusion of fish and bird on the gold band skillfully integrated two clan symbols, "fish" and "bird," into one. Did it symbolize the marriage of the two clans and thus formed a new Shu clan symbol? Was this peculiar combination of fish and birds, with its strong totemic connotations, intended as a clearer and more straightforward expression of the intimate solidarity between two clans who worshipped fish and birds as symbols of their ancestral gods? Did the combination of the images, which appeared to be fierce, suggest the power of the two clans after their alliance? Did the more outward arrangement of the fish's tails, as opposed to the long beaks, also suggest the unity of the two clans after their alliance? Did the novel image of a conjoined fish and bird symbolize the transformation of the fish clan into the bird clan? Records of *Biographies of the King of Shu* seemed to reveal this kind of information. In short, the unique patterns contain rich connotations and bring us a wealth of associations. It is likely that the Yufu clan in the Ancient Shu Dynasty was probably a clan with fish and birds as its ancestral gods, or a royal clan composed of two clans, and its "Yufu" clan symbol might also be a combination of patterns.

The gold crown band and gold bands excavated at the Jinsha site were used by the powerful and distinguished members of the Ancient Shu clan and the elaborate designs and decorations on them are likely to have been of an exclusive nature. The patterns of birds' heads and fish's bodies on the gold bands are similar to those on the gold crown band and can be regarded as a unique "image language." They were all created by the Ancient Shu people through their rich imagination and were very different from the culture revealed by archaeological finds in other regions, fully demonstrating the romantic and distinctive style of the Ancient Shu period. These patterns, unique and mysterious, still have an extraordinary charm today.

Bronze figurine with a man's head and a bird's body from the Sanxingdui site

7

———◦◦◇◦◦———

Tiger-Worshipping Tribe

When we look at these stone tigers today, what we feel and experience is more than the profound connotations behind them. Their artistic charm travels through time and space and evokes our imagination and resonance.

Among the large number of cultural relics unearthed at the Jinsha site, there are many stone tigers. Crafted with refined techniques, they appear vivid and can be regarded as masterpieces among the round stone sculptures in the Shang and Zhou dynasties.

According to the published archaeological data, the stone tigers were all in a prone position. Each of them was made of a whole stone into a primary shape and then was carefully polished. Thus, they were unique in shape and distinctive in style. With skilled craftsmanship, the tiger's crouching posture and open-mouthed roar have been vividly depicted. In addition, the use of stones, some of which are gray-yellow peridotite and some of which are gray-black serpentine, adds to the vividness of these round-carved tigers. Because the natural color and stripes of these stones were similar to the tiger pattern, an unexpected sense of wonder was created. The tigers appeared realistic in form and appearance, reflecting the maker's meticulous observation of the king of beasts in nature and showing a high level of carving skill and imitation ability. The maker also applied vermilion to the eyes, ears, and

Stone tigers unearthed at the Jinsha site

mouths of the tigers, suggesting that they may have been closely associated with Ancient Shu rituals. These stone tiger sculptures reveal rich information about the worship and aesthetic taste of the Ancient Shu people and make us know their awe and respect for the tiger.

One of the tigers (No. 2001CQJC: 211) measures 28.44 cm in length, 8.94 cm in width, 19.88 cm in height, and weighs 5,457 g. Engraved from serpentinite whose grayish-white stripes resemble those of real tigers, the tiger appears lifelike and intriguing. It is in a crouching posture, with its head held high and its mouth wide open in the shape of a roaring tiger. Its neck and head are relatively stout, and the four sharp canine teeth are exposed in its wide-open mouth. With its front and hind paws bent forward, and its hips slightly bent, the tiger seems ready to strike, vividly representing the majesty and power of the king of beasts. On the hip of the tiger, there is a small round hole, which should be used to install its tail. The tail may have been carved from a separate piece of stone, but unfortunately, no remains have been unearthed. In terms of the carving process, the stone tiger is likely to be first made of stone into a rough shape and then carved and polished. The tiger mouth may have adopted the method of a pipe drilling technique, while the head was

Stone qing (a percussion instrument)
unearthed at Wuguan Village in
Anyang, Henan Province

Gold tiger unearthed at the
Sanxingdui site

Jade tiger excavated at the Yinxu site
in Anyang, Henan Province

Jade tiger unearthed at the Western Zhou
tomb in Beiyao, Luoyang, Henan Province

finely carved, highlighting its rugged style and delicate features. Finally, the tiger's mouth, eyes, and ears are painted with vermilion, which seems to have been used as a finishing touch, reinforcing the symbolism of the tiger and adding a sense of mystery.

Another stone tiger (No. 2001CQJC: 684) weighs 5,644 g, with a length of 28.8 cm, a width of 8.42 cm, and a height of 21.5 cm. It is carved out of grayish-yellow serpentined peridotite. When unearthed, its right foreleg was broken, and the left one is slightly damaged, which was restored after splicing. Like the tiger mentioned above, this one was in a prone position too. The strong hind legs, sturdy neck, wide mouth, and sharp teeth demonstrate the power of the tiger. It is vividly carved and carefully polished. Its large mouth also adopts drilling technology, as is the round hole in the rump for the tiger's tail. The lines around the mouth, the diamond-shaped eyes, the whiskers on either side of the nose, and the almond-shaped ears at the back of the head are all delicately carved. The combination of realistic and exaggerated techniques and the application of concise lines make the tiger rough and dignified, which is evocative. Moreover, the tiger's mouth, eyes, and ears are similarly coated with vermilion and the traces of which are still clearly visible, although it has been buried for thousands of years.

The environmental archaeological material suggests that tigers may have been frequent in the mountains and forests of the Sichuan Basin during the Shang and Zhou periods and that many ancient tribes in the southwest worshipped them as totems. Using various materials to represent tigers and convey their awe for the animal was probably one of the more popular practices of the Ancient Shu. For example, the gold tiger and tiger-shaped bronze vessels unearthed in the pit No. 1 of the Sanxingdui site also reflect the ancients' reverence for tigers. The gold tiger was also depicted with its mouth wide open, eyes hollowed out, ears erect, tail curled upward, body curved like a silkworm, and limbs crouched and ready to jump. The tiger-shaped bronze vessel also features a raised head, an upturned tail, rounded eyes, visible teeth, and strong limbs in a crouching position, which, through its unique modeling is a powerful and fearsome expression of the tiger. Both of them and the stone tiger excavated from the Jinsha site are created with a combination of realistic and exaggerated technique; whether it is the use of materials or the creativity of the shape, they are extremely ingenious and have the distinct characteristics of the regional culture.

Stone and jade tigers of Shang and Zhou dynasties were also unearthed in other areas, but their features are different from those of the Ancient Shu. Their body, head and tail are mostly flattened out, with a strong emphasis on resemblance, as in the case of the jade and stone tigers excavated at the Yinxu site in Anyang, Henan Province, and the jade tiger excavated from the Western Zhou tomb in Beiyao, Luoyang, Henan Province. These tigers' heads are flattened out, their tails trailed behind them, and their bodies are carved with ornaments, which may have been a more popular style in the Central Plains. In contrast, the stone tigers excavated at the Jinsha site, without exception, are all roaring with their heads raised, which make them more vivid and majestic. Notably, a Chinese instrument called qing from the late Shang Dynasty was unearthed at Wuguan Village in Anyang, Henan Province, which also depicted a tiger roaring with its mouth open and teeth exposed, and there was a magnificent ornament on the body of the tiger. The tiger's head, however, is still stretched forward and its mouth opened wide downward, making the whole tiger prostrate. Researchers believe that the stone qing with tiger patterns was a ceremonial instrument used by royal family of Yin and that it was a noble instrument dedicated to ritual activities such as sacrificial ceremonies, imperial ceremonies, and feasts for the aristocrats. The depiction of tiger patterns on them is likely to be related to tiger worship at that time. Stone tigers excavated at the Jinsha site also reflect the Ancient Shu's reverence for the tiger, and their reverence appears to have been more solemn and intense than that of the Yin.

Another difference lies in their functions. Most of the stone tigers, jade tigers, and stone qing with tiger motifs unearthed in the Central Plains and other places were things used by the dead or objects buried with the dead. However, the gold tigers, bronze tigers, and stone tigers unearthed at the Sanxingdui site and the Jinsha site were related to sacrificial activities of the Ancient Shu people. The cinnabar painted on the stone tiger may also be a unique custom of the Ancient Shu people. Some special bronze sculptures unearthed at the Sanxingdui site, such as the vertical-eyed bronze mask, bronze human head, and bronze masks were all coated with cinnabar on the lips. It suggested these stone tigers unearthed at the Jinsha site are likely to be important offerings in temples or shrines of Ancient Shu or instruments used in major sacrifices.

It is likely that the Ancient Shu people, with the Jinsha site as the center of their accommodation and activities, were made up of several tribes and clans. Among them, there were tribes that worshipped birds and fish, as well as tribes that worshipped tigers. They may have married each other or formed alliances, resulting in the growing strength of the Jinsha tribes. The numerous stone tigers unearthed at the Jinsha site indicate that the tiger worship tribe occupied an important position in the Ancient Shu. These stone tigers were symbols of these tribes' reverence for tigers. It is worth noting that the reverence for tigers is also reflected in numerous other artifacts excavated from the Jinsha site, such as two jade zhang blades (No. 2001CQJC: 136 and No. 2001CQJC: 955). The animal decoration carved on the bolster sections of the two jade zhang blades is probably in the form of a tiger. The beast's face, depicted

The jade Zhang unearthed from the Jinsha site is carved with tiger-shaped decorations on its handle.

73

Bronze animal-face object unearthed at the Jinsha site

Bronze tiger unearthed at the Jinsha site

on the jade-ax-shaped vessel with exposed teeth and rounded eyes, is also an evocative portrayal of the majesty of the tiger's head. In addition, a bronze tiger unearthed at the Jinsha site, according to archaeologists, is almost the same in form and shape as the bronze tiger unearthed at the Sanxingdui site. Moreover, four bronze animal faces have also been excavated from the Jinsha site. They represent the head shapes of the tiger vividly. Although the designs of these excavated artifacts are diverse, they all embody worship of the tiger.

Documentary records and archaeological discoveries suggest that the Chinese nation has long had the concept and custom of worshipping tigers and that it was widespread, especially in the southwest and among some ancient tribes in the middle and upper reaches of the Yangtze River. The earliest artifacts excavated can be traced back to more than 6,000 years ago. There were tiger patterns and dragon patterns shaped from clam shells in the tombs of the Xishuipo site in Puyang, Henan Province, which is likely to be related to the custom of tiger and dragon worship of the tomb owners. The long-standing custom of tiger worship may have had a very important relationship with the hunting activities of the ancestors and their living environment. In ancient times, tiger worship was a common practice among the tribes of the Hengduan Mountains in the west of China, from Gansu and Qinghai in the north to Yunnan and Qianxi in the south. This is especially true of the southwestern tribes from the ancient Diqiang families. They worshipped either the white tiger or the black tiger. This traditional practice of tiger worship has had a significant impact on the cultures of the southwestern tribes and even on Chinese culture as a whole and has survived for thousands of years in the cultures of the Yi, Naxi, Bai, Tujia, and other southwestern minority groups.

In particular, the Ba tribe, who were closely related to the Shu tribe, also worshipped the tiger. According to the *Book of the Later Han*, Lin Jun,

LEFT Bronze zheng carved with one tiger, and three stars of the Zhou Dynasty unearthed in Guanghan, Sichuan Province (in the collection of the Sichuan Museum)

ABOVE LEFT Bronze tiger object unearthed at the Sanxingdui site

ABOVE RIGHT Bronze chunyu with tiger-shaped handling —the collection of the Sichuan Museum

elected as chieftain over five native tribes of Ba, transformed into a white tiger after his death. This is also recorded in the *Book of the Man Barbarians* by Fan Chuo. Therefore, the Ba people took the white tiger as an object of worship and regarded themselves as descendants of the white tiger. Although these records are of a legendary nature, some of them were corroborated by archaeological discoveries. Most Ba artifacts excavated since the mid-20th century are decorated with tiger patterns. Chunyu (an ancient musical instrument) also has tiger-shaped handles and Ba-style bronze dagger-axes with tiger motifs unearthed in Ba tombs. Not only are there carvings of tigers on the tiger-shaped handles, but also vivid tiger patterns are engraved on weapons, such as the copper zheng and copper ge, which are obviously reflections of the ancient Ba people's custom of venerating tigers. These are clearly a reflection of the ancient Ba's custom of tiger worship. Two bronze chunyu from the Warring States period are in the collection of the Sichuan Provincial Museum. The "tigers" on their tops are standing with heads raised, and tails curled. Scholars speculate that they may be the relics of ancient Ba princes and lords. In the Chu tombs in the Jiangling area of Hubei, wooden lacquer wares such as the tiger and phoenix drum and a carving of a phoenix standing on the back of a lying tiger have been unearthed. These lacquer wares are all in the design of a tall phoenix standing on the back of a tiger lying on the ground. As the phoenix is the totem of the ancient Chu and the Ba people take the tiger as their totem, scholars believe that these artifacts suggest that the Chu people respect the phoenix but devalue the tiger. As we can see, the Ba people's tiger worship has a significant influence in the middle reaches of the Yangtze River and the surrounding areas.

The Yi, who was also closely related to the Ancient Shu, had a tradition of tiger worship too, but their totem is the black tiger. In the *Classic of Areas Overseas · the North of the Classic of Mountains and Seas*, there is a record that "a green beast, with the shape of a tiger, is called Luoluo." So far, the barbarians in Yunnan Province still call the tiger Luoluo, while the Yi people call the tiger Luo and call themselves "Luoluo," with the men calling themselves "Luoluopo" or "Luopo" and the women calling themselves "Luoluomo" or "Luomo." It is clear that the Yi people regard themselves as a tribe of tigers. The green tiger mentioned in the *Classic of Mountains and Seas*, Luoluo, is the black tiger totem of the Yi people. Among the bronze artifacts excavated from ancient sites such as Shizhai Mountain in Jinning and Lijiashan in Jiangchuan, Yunnan, there are many physical examples of tiger totem worship. It proves that tiger worship was once prevalent in the ancient southwest. As we can see that the worship of the tiger or the use of the tiger as a totem was indeed quite common in southwest China in ancient times. However, due to differences in ethnicity and customs, some tribes took the white tiger as their ancestor, while others regarded the black tiger as their ancestor. The Ba people worshipped the white tiger while the Yi worshipped the black tiger, showing their different characteristics.

The Ancient Shu also had the custom of worshipping "green." The ancient literature says that the king of Shu, Cancong, was called "the god in green." There are bronze tigers with turquoise inlays throughout their body unearthed at the Sanxingdui site. Most of the bronze statues had eyebrows and eyes painted black, while most of the stone tigers unearthed at the Jinsha site were made of gray and black stones or stones with cyan markings. All of these show the Ancient Shu people's reverence for black. Nevertheless, there are also gold tigers at the Sanxingdui site and yellowish stone tigers at the Jinsha site. According to the *Records of the Huayang Kingdom · Records of Shu*, the ninth king of the Kaiming Dynasty began to reverence the color red and

Bronze dagger-axe with tiger pattern,
image language and inscriptions of Bashu
unearthed in Pidu District, Chengdu

Bronze dagger-axe with tiger pattern
unearthed at Baihuatan Middle School,
Chengdu

the five colors (blue, red, black, yellow, and white) were still used as ancestral tablets and temple titles after the death of the king of Shu, reflecting the diversity of color revered among the Ancient Shu. It is likely that reverence of color among tiger-worshipping tribes in the Ancient Shu was not confined to black or white, and their tiger-worshipping traditions are highly inclusive. While stone tigers excavated at the Jinsha site are vivid, distinctive, and numerous, there are very few bronze statues, which is intriguing. In terms of time, the Jinsha site was slightly later than and immediately after the Sanxingdui site. When the ancient city of Sanxingdui was still the capital of the thriving kingdom, Jinsha had already been an important tribal habitat for the Ancient Shu Kingdom. Can we make a conjecture that the Jinsha people used bronze statues in their rituals because of the influence of Sanxingdui, but the use of the stone tiger as a symbol of ritual and worship was a long-standing tradition of their own? The tiger-worshipping Shu tribes that inhabited the Jinsha site were, for a long time, under the authority of the royal capital of Sanxingdui. It is likely that after the sudden decline and annihilation of Sanxingdui, a considerable number of Shu people migrated and merged with the increasingly powerful tiger-worshipping tribes at the Jinsha site, making it a new and prosperous place after Sanxingdui. It is probably for this reason that the Jinsha site is particularly diverse in culture. In addition to the worship of the stone tiger, sun worship flourished, and there were activities such as "worshipping the sun for rain," among others.

A large number of stone tigers not only reflects the prevalence of tiger worship in the Jinsha site but also reveals that these stone tigers may have a close relationship with the Ancient Shu people's concept of worshipping stones, both of which held a very important place in the minds of the rulers of the Jinsha site. As we know, in ancient times, there was a legend that "Yu was born from a stone," and his son, Qi, broke the stone and was born. There is still a custom of worshipping the blood stone near Yu's Cave in Beichuan.

Stone worship by the Xia people had an important influence on many Qiang language ethnic groups and some Tibeto-Burman languages ethnic groups in the southwest. The Qiang people had the custom of white stone worship, which has continued to this day. The history of stone worship among the Ancient Shu people has also been long. *Records of the Huayang Kingdom · Records of Shu* said that after the death of Chancong, the first king in Ancient Shu, "People made a stone coffin for him, and people in the country followed this custom." It also said that during the reign of Kaiming, another king of Ancient Shu, "every time a king died, a large stone, three feet long and weighing a thousand pounds, was erected as tomb memorial, the present stalagmite," which revealed the Ancient Shu's original religious consciousness of stone worship, and the fact that stone worship was still prevalent in the Chengdu Plain after the Ancient Shu moved out of Minshan Mountain and settled there. The opening of the Shiniu Road in the late Kaiming Dynasty, and the Stone Man and Stone Rhinoceros carved by Li Bing for flood control, were related to stone worship by the Ancient Shu as well. The large number of stone sculptures excavated from the Jinsha site, such as stone kneeling figures and stone tigers, suggest that the ruling tribe in the Jinsha site enjoys a tradition of stone worship and tiger worship. The elaborately carved stone tigers are thus the product of a fusion of tiger worship and stone worship.

The Stone tigers unearthed at the Jinsha site and the worship customs they embodied have also had a great influence on later generations. We can see a portrait of Xiwangmu sitting on the dragon and tiger throne from the Han Dynasty stone and brick unearthed in Sichuan. The shape of the tiger, with its head raised and mouth open, is very similar to that of the stone tiger unearthed at the Jinsha site. However, on the portrait stones and bricks excavated in Henan, Jiangsu, and Shandong provinces, Xi Wang Mu is mostly seated on platforms or square thrones, which are quite different from portraits in Ancient Shu. We know that there is a dragon on the bronze sacred tree of the Sanxingdui site and a stone tiger unearthed at the Jinsha site, both of which were the Ancient Shu people's symbols of worship during the Shang and Zhou periods. The Shu people of later generations skilfully transformed the two into the dragon and tiger throne of Xi Wang Mu,

Portrait of Xiwangmu (Queen Mother of the West) on a stone coffin of the Han Dynasty unearthed in Pengshan, Sichuan Province

Flying tiger driving for Lei Gong (god of Thunder) on a stone of the Han Dynasty unearthed in Nanyang, Henan Province

Portrait of Xiwangmu sitting on the dragon and tiger throne on a brick of the Han Dynasty unearthed in Xinfan, Sichuan Province

which was be a creative play in faith worship. To put it more profoundly, the dragon and tiger thrones on the portrait stones and bricks of Xi Wang Mu in the Ancient Shu during the Han Dynasty are not only the remnants of dragon worship and tiger worship during the Shang and Zhou periods but also a promotion of its traditional customs and spiritual concepts. It is worth mentioning that the representation of tigers in the Han Dynasty portraits is quite rich, including the impressive dragon and tiger throne of Xi Wang Mu, the flying tiger driving for Lei Gong (the god of thunder), the winged divine tiger, and the immortal riding on a tiger. Some of the portraits also depict the image of "expelling demons and epidemic diseases with tigers" and "tigers eating the goddess of drought," indicating that the worship of the tiger has evolved in later times.

The stone tiger excavated at the Jinsha site not only reveals much information about the Ancient Shu, but also gives us more insight. When we look at these stone tigers today, what we feel and experience is more than the profound connotations behind them. Their artistic charm, and travels through time and space evoke our imagination and resonance.

8

———◇◇◇◇◇———

Stone Witches

All these stone kneeling figures are like suffering. Something in their eyes begins to shed, like sadness, but with silence, expectation, supplication, waiting, depression, and surprise as well.

Many amazing discoveries have been made at the Jinsha site. The numerous stone figures are one of the masterpieces the Ancient Shu made in figure-making. Both the skillful simplicity of the carving technique and the unique and mysterious style of the form are like a breath of fresh air. A total of eight stone figure statues were initially unearthed, which, together with those excavated later, eventually amounted to more than ten pieces. The unique posture and distinctive form of these stone figures have given rise to speculation among scholars since they were unearthed. What is the identity behind their special postures? What symbolic meaning was given to them? And what role did they play in the rituals of the Ancient Shu? These are all very interesting questions worth exploring.

During our visit to the cultural relics unearthed at the Jinsha site, we noticed that all the stone figures were in the shape of something kneeling. Without exception, they were all nude, kneeling with both knees on the ground and their hips on their heels, barefoot and without shoes and socks. This naked shape appears bold and open, displaying a mysterious allegory and special style. Their hands are crossed behind their backs, and their wrists are tied by rope, some with two or more bindings of rope. Their palms are

FAR LEFT Stone kneeling figure excavated at the Jinsha site

LEFT Stone kneeling figure excavated at Fangchi Street, Chengdu

spread downward, with their fingers pressed against the backs of their hips. Such a pose is very intriguing and probably has an unusual meaning. The hairstyle of these stone kneeling figures is also quite peculiar, as they appear to have a special tile on the top of their heads, and the shape of the low concave middle rising to the sides resembles an open book, giving them a very strange appearance. They have no hair on their forehead or temples, and the back of the head is carved in lines to show the long, trailing braids, which are four cords of double strands falling in parallel to the back of the head, the lower end of which is covered by the hands tied backward. The long braids at the back of the heads of the figures would be typical of the Ancient Shu tradition, as many of the bronze human heads and standing figures excavated at the Sanxingdui site have long braids behind their heads, as is the case with the bronze standing figures and the stone kneeling figures at the Jinsha site. However, there are two stone kneeling figures without braided lines on the back of their heads, presumably because the stone figures had not been further processed and carved after the stone figures had been carved into shape or because the carving was shallow and indecipherable due to their age.

In carving techniques and modeling, these stone kneeling figures are characterized by their simplicity and boldness. The makers combined circular carving with line engraving, integrating realism and exaggeration, to make the figures vivid and evocative. Compared with the bronze statues of the Sanxingdui site, these stone kneeling figures differ in form, pose, and decorative features, as well as in the choice of materials and aesthetic tastes. Most of these stone kneeling figures have high cheekbones, a high nose, a wide forehead, and a prominent eyebrow arch. With their almond eyes open wide, they have their eyes and pupils carved into a forward stare. They enjoy large ears, with pierced earlobes. The lower side of their faces is thin, and their cheeks are slightly concave. Their mouths are either pursed or open, and some with traces of vermilion on the lips and ears. Particular attention is drawn to their expressions and demeanor, all of which look like they are suffering, full of sadness, but with silence, expectation, supplication, waiting, depression, and surprise. This not only demonstrates the skill of the carver but also reflects his careful observation and mastery of the expressions of the figures at the time. The expressions of these stone figures, as well as the solemn and mysterious appearance of the bronze figures at the Jinsha site, may all express a kind of allegorical meaning. It is obvious that the traces of vermilion applied to the lips and ears of the stone figures were made by the Ancient Shu when they held sacrificial activities. The application of vermilion is likely to be related to witchcraft, as people do this to enhance the efficacy of spiritual power and exorcism. But it might just be a specific ritual practice of the Ancient Shu as well.

Looking back at the archaeological discoveries in Sichuan since the 20th century, two stone kneeling figures have been unearthed from the Sanxingdui site. Unfortunately, their heads have been damaged, their shapes and expressions are unknown, and the carvings on their bodies are indecipherable. However, the kneeling position with hands tied behind the back is still vaguely recognizable. In 1983, a stone kneeling figure was also unearthed at the site of Fangchi Street in Chengdu. According to the published archaeological data, it is a lapis lazuli sculpture, about 50 cm high, and the shape is also naked. Both hands are tied behind the back, and both legs are kneeling on the ground. The head is large, the face is rough, the cheekbones are high, the forehead is protruding, the ears are upright, the nose is high, the mouth is wide, the face is relatively thin and long, and the hair is divided from the middle to the left and right, and the look is serious and sad. Based on the contact relationship of strata and excavated materials, it can be judged that the carving and use of these stone kneeling figures also date to the Shang and Zhou periods. Their modeling style and morphological characteristics are very similar to those of the stone kneeling figures excavated at the Jinsha site, and their expressions are consistent and highly coherent. No similar finds have been made in the numerous archaeological excavations conducted over the years in other areas outside of Sichuan. Obviously, these stone figures are typical of Ancient Shu relics, with distinct contemporary and strong regional cultural characteristics, and are mainly distributed in some of the larger ancient sites of the Shang and Zhou periods on the Chengdu Plain. It is certain that the Ancient Shu people did not carve these stone figures for the purpose of enjoyment, as modern people do in the production of handicrafts, and the characteristic style of these stone figures fully illustrates that the carvers did not pursue visual pleasure, but deliberately expressed a strong tragic power. The use of hard stone to carve these stone kneeling figures with special symbolic meanings was probably a special ritual in the Ancient Shu Kingdom during the Shang and Zhou periods. Or perhaps these stone kneeling figures were carved by some larger clans or tribes in the Ancient Shu Kingdom for ritual purpose, and they were given a special symbolic meaning.

Archaeologists roughly divided the stone kneeling figures at the Jinsha site into three types, A, B, and C, based on their modeling characteristics. Of these, type A is thinner, with the upper body leaning slightly forward and the features carved in a relatively crude manner, standing approximately 17 cm high. Type C is larger, with a straighter and slightly flatter upper body, wider shoulders, and exaggerated in some parts, about 21–27 cm high. In comparison, type B and type C are more detailed and beautifully carved, while type A is cruder.

Let's now look at some of the published stone kneeling figures.

The first stone figure (No. 2001CQJC: 716) is the most meticulously carved and well-preserved one among the dozen or so stone kneeling figures excavated at the Jinsha site. It is 21.72 cm in height and 2,117 g in weight. The carver used carving, polishing, drilling, and line engraving to make a vivid and realistic representation of it, and applied color and vermilion to some parts of the face. Some parts are exaggerated and abbreviated, displaying a distinctive and rugged style. In particular, its linearly carved eyes, dilated pupils, square mouth with drooping corners and vermilion-painted lips, concave cheeks and high nose, erect round ears and drilled earlobes, strange middle parting hairstyle, large braids drooping at the back of the head and back-bound hands, as well as the kneeling position with both knees on the ground, all give people a sense of vividness. The stone chosen for this statue is serpentinite peridotite, which contains powdered iron ore, forming some yellow-brown spots on the surface of the statue, which, together with the artificial color painting and vermilion on the face, adds to the antiquity and

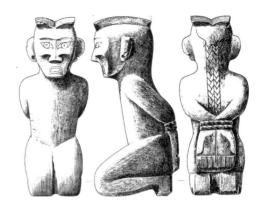

Stone kneeling figure No. 2001CQJC: 716 excavated at the Jinsha site and its line drawing

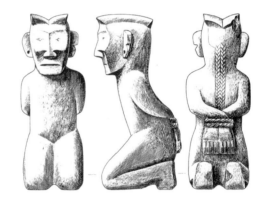

Stone kneeling figure No. 2001CQJC: 717 excavated at the Jinsha site and its line drawing

mystery of this stone statue. Judging from the physical features, this stone kneeling figure is a nude male kneeling with hands tied behind his back. Its facial expression is of seriousness, bitterness, and astonishment, with eyes wide open and a wide mouth open with drooping corners, which seems to contain complex meanings of sadness, indignation, expectation, and prayer. The hands tied behind him by two ropes appear to be exaggerated, probably intentionally, to highlight the allegorical meaning expressed by his hands bound behind him.

The second stone figure (No. 2001CQJC: 717), 21.5 cm in height and 1,951 g in weight, is also an exquisite and delicate carving. This stone kneeling figure is also carved with the techniques of round carving and line engraving, and its body appears plump, stable, and balanced. The stone used is also serpentinite peridotite, as it contains powdered iron ore and calcite, which gives the stone a brownish patina with black streaks and white scratches after erosion, adding a natural charm to the figure. In addition, due to weathering of the stone over time, small cracks have appeared on its body. In terms of form, the stone statue also focuses on strange hairstyle and kneeling posture with hands tied behind the back, wide-open eyes, clear facial edges, raised cheekbones, concaved cheeks, high and straight nose, pursed mouth, solemn and serious expression. Its face also implies subtle changes such as sadness, bitterness, and expectation. The carver also used color painting to render and enhance the expression. For example, the eyes are painted black, the eyelids are painted with vermilion, and the eyeballs are white, all making the figure fully expressive. In particular, the vermilion painted on the tightly pursed broad mouth was still as bright as new when it was unearthed after thousands of years of oblivion. The painting and vermilion application not only reflect the unique aesthetic sense of the Ancient Shu people but are probably related to the ritual practices and religious concepts of the time.

The third stone kneeling figure (No. 2001CQJC: 166) is 17.4 cm high and weighs 1148 g. It is carved from light grayish-black marble, with more white streaks. Some parts of the figure were mutilated when excavated, the head having been disconnected from the body, which was restored by splicing. This stone statue is also characterized by high cheekbones, a thin face, a middle parting hairstyle, a forward-leaning body, a serious expression, and a mournful demeanor. The carver also used techniques, such as round carving, line engraving, polishing, and painting, but the fine details of the statue, especially the facial features and the hands tied behind the body, are rougher. Its body is slightly smaller than other stone statues, and its hands and feet are thinner. The part above the nose bridge of this stone statue is not carefully carved. The hands are crossed behind the back, and the ropes tied to the hands are only in outline, with seven carved fingers and no carved hair braid behind the body. In general, the work is rather crude. Could the need for it be so urgent that it could not be carved in time? It may also be an early style of carving. However, the vermilion applied to its mouth and eyes clearly indicate that this stone statue was already used in rituals of the Ancient Shu or as an offering in the clan temples or shrines of the rulers of the Jinsha site.

The fourth stone kneeling figure (No. 2001CQJC: 159) is 17.8 cm high, weighing 1,366 g. It is carved from serpentine lapis lazuli which is more common in Pengzhou in the western part of the Chengdu Plain. Could

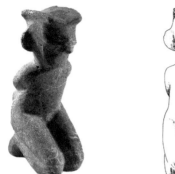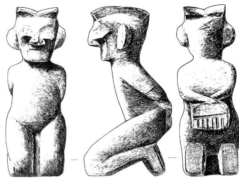

Stone kneeling figure No. 2001CQJC: 166 excavated at the Jinsha site and its line drawing

Stone kneeling figure No. 2001CQJC: 159 excavated at the Jinsha site and its line drawing

the stone used by the Ancient Shu people have been quarried here? The stone statue has a large number of yellow spots on its chest and legs. It was broken when unearthed and restored after splicing. In the style of modeling, it also has a thin face, prominent cheekbones, a middle parting hairstyle, a forward-looking gaze, and a solemn and mournful expression. Its form is similar to that of the third one, and its carving is rough, especially the part above the nose. A convex ridge is used above the eye to show the thick and long eyebrows. The hands tied behind him are also roughly carved, with only five fingers carved. The bottom of the kneeling legs is uneven and slightly tilted to the left when placed. This stone statue is apparently only a prototype and has not been further processed, but there are also traces of painting and vermilion left which suggests it was used in rituals.

What do these kneeling figures unearthed from the Jinsha site represented? What identities do they symbolize? These unsolved problems have attracted the attention of scholars. Some speculate that these stone kneeling figures may represent the lower class of the society at that time, suggesting that they would have belonged to a low-status group within Ancient Shu, while others think that they may represent people from other races, who are prisoners of war or slaves and so on. Others even believe that these large number of unearthed stone kneeling figures may reflect the system of hierarchy and punishments of the Ancient Shu or the Kingdom at that time, or they may be substitutes for human sacrifices. Most of these conjectures are based on the shape of the kneeling stone statues with their hands bound behind their backs.

On closer examination, we can see that these speculations are not accurate. The first is the theory of punishment. Whether it is the *"Yu Xing"* of the Xia Dynasty (2070–1600 BC) or the *"Tang Law"* of the Shang Dynasty described in the *Bamboo Annals* and *Records of the Grand Historian · the Yin Dynasty*, haircut and hands tied behind are not explicitly defined as five punishments. The Ancient Shu Kingdom was composed of many clans and tribes, with a co-ownership system in politics and self-contained rituals and music. There is almost no record of its penal system in ancient documents or archaeological literature, so we do not yet know what the penal system was like in Ancient Shu or whether it had a distinctive penal system. Second, the theory of substitutes for human sacrifice is probably difficult to substantiate. Human sacrifice and burying the living with the dead were once widely adopted by the rulers of the Yin-Shang Dynasty in the Central Plains, especially in the late Shang Dynasty. There are many records of this in oracle bone inscriptions and ancient documents. The funerary practices of the Ancient Shu Kingdom were very different from those of the Central Plains dynasties. Many major archaeological excavations, such as those at the Sanxingdui site and the Jinsha site, did not find any human sacrifices or the living buried in the tombs of the Ancient Shu rulers. It can be seen that the kneeling stone figures unearthed at the Jinsha site do not represent a substitute for human sacrifice, nor can they reveal the penal practices in the Ancient Shu Kingdom. The postures of the naked hands bound behind their backs are not intended to represent a penal practice but are endowed with special symbolic meanings, which are obviously related to some special sacrificial ceremonies of the Ancient Shu.

LEFT Bronze kneeling figure topped with a zun excavated from the Sanxingdui site

ABOVE Bronze kneeling figure excavated from the Sanxingdui site

So, were these stone kneeling figures of very low status? As we know, kneeling was a ritual for the ruling class during the Yin-Shang Dynasty, and it was also the etiquette when worshipping ancestors, offering sacrifices to gods and heaven, and entertaining guests. Some round-carved jade figures and stone figures unearthed from the tomb of Fuhao in the Yin Ruins are in kneeling postures. Among them is a beautifully carved and delicately decorated jade figure of the Shang Dynasty. Some people speculate that it may be the image of Fuhao herself based on the demeanor and the weapon she wears. Among the bronze statues unearthed at the Sanxingdui site, many are kneeling postures. The kneeling posture, whether at the Yin Ruins or the Sanxingdui site, does not represent the low-status ethnic groups, but the upper-class figures in society. They may be the ruling class, secular nobles, or witches who wielded divine power. Taking it as a reference, the stone kneeling figures excavated at the Jinsha site, without exception, adopted the kneeling posture used to represent upper-class noble figures in the Central Plains in the Shang and Zhou dynasties. Obviously, they also showed the etiquette and customs of the upper-class figures in society. All these suggest that they are not figures with low social status but rather symbols of ruling class figures. It is very likely that they could be the image of a clan or tribal leader or witch in a sacrificial ceremony in the Ancient Shu Kingdom.

The hands of these stone kneeling figures, which are bound backward with ropes, also demand special attention, as do their oddly trimmed hairstyles, which seem to have been given a specific yet clear meaning. This leads us readily to relevant ancient documentation. According to *Master Lü's Spring and Autumn Annals · Shunmin*, during the Shang Dynasty, there was a time when the world was in a severe drought and had no harvests for five years. Tang, the supreme ruler of the Shang Dynasty, prayed in the mulberry forest with his body as a sacrifice. "He cut his hair, rubbed his hands, and sacrificed his body to the gods in a prayer of blessing, and the people were very happy; then, it began to pour rain." There were similar accounts in *Mozi · Universal Love, Discourses of the States · Zhou Yu, Shizi · Chuozi, Huainanzi*, etc. "翦其发" mentioned in these books means to cut hair into a strange hairstyle. "酈其手," according to Bi Yuan, Yu Yue, Chen Qiyou, and others, means to bind ten fingers with a wooden handle. It was a ritual held by the rulers of the Shang Dynasty in times of great drought, the purpose of which was to sacrifice to the sun and the gods and to pray for good weather and peace and prosperity in the country. Praying for rain due to a severe drought was once an important ritual during the Shang and Zhou dynasties. There were mainly two ways of praying for rain during the Shang Dynasty: one was to pray for rain by dancing, and the other was to pray for rain by burning witches.

The practice of praying for rain by dancing in the Shang Dynasty was a ritual of praying for rain by playing music and dancing. Sometimes it was held for consecutive days or even with the king dancing for rain as his own. In the Shang Dynasty, burning witches for rain was a ritual to pray for rain when the drought was particularly severe. There are a lot of records in historical books and oracle bone inscriptions. Some oracle bones recorded several places where more than one witch was burned at the same time, while some recorded several witches were burned within a few days. When drought is particularly severe, those with higher status could also be sacrificed, as in the case of Shang Tang's desire to burn himself in sacrifice. The practice still existed in the Zhou Dynasty but gradually evolved from burning witches to exposing witches to the sun for rain. Some scholars believe that the "Corpse of Nvchou" or "Corpse of Huangji" described in the *Classic of Mountains and Seas* may have been sacrificial offerings exposed to the sun to pray for rain during the long drought in ancient times. Also, being naked is a practice of praying for rain by imitating witchcraft of interacting between heaven and humans, a practice that was not only prevalent in ancient China but also in many other parts of the world, as is authentically documented in Fraser's *Golden Bough*.

From this perspective, these stone kneeling figures excavated at the Jinsha site, with the shape of "cutting hair" and "binding fingers," had the allegorical meaning of "sacrificing the body to pray for god," which is obviously the portrayal of "exposing witches to the sun for rain." When the Yin "burned witches to pray for rain," what they burned were the living, and when the people of Zhou "exposed witches to the sun for rain," what they exposed to the scorching sun were the living, too. The use of stone kneeling figures to symbolize and replace witches would have been a practice with strong Ancient Shu characteristics, and its nature is in line with that of the bronze statues at the Sanxingdui site. It suggests that the sacrificial activities under the co-dominant political order of the Ancient Shu were different from those in the Central Plains and had their unique characteristics. These witches carved out of stones have a lot to do with the concept of stone worship in the Ancient Shu, and we could take them as the product of the stone worship tradition. The Ancient Shu's concept of communication between gods and human is also well reflected in these stone kneeling figures. The application of vermilion to the faces of the stone kneeling figures may be the finishing touch in witchcraft, which symbolizes that the Ancient Shu people injected mysterious power into these stone statues, making them the incarnation of real witches who can communicate with gods.

The stone figures unearthed at the Jinsha site inspire us in many ways. The creative and imaginative craftsmen of the Ancient Shu period carved hard stones into figures of witches, which, apart from the reverence for tradition and the need for ritual activities, was also closely related to the fact that the Ancient Shu excelled in figure sculpture. Many ancient peoples in the world had a tradition of carving stones into figures, for example, well-known ancient Egypt, ancient Greece, and ancient Rome. The Ancient Shu people were no less impressive. These masterpieces of stone figures unearthed from the Jinsha site are as irreplaceable as the bronze statues unearthed from the Sanxingdui site. They not only reflect the brilliance of the Ancient Shu civilization but write a new chapter in the history of world art as well.

9

—◦◦◇◦◦—

Jade Cong from the Archaeological Ruins of Liangzhu City

One key contributing factor behind the diversity of Shu culture and prosperity of the Shu community is the exchange and innovation of the Ancient Shu people.

Archaeological findings tell us that, since ancient times, it is an age-old tradition for Chinese people to make and use jade objects. As early as five thousand years ago in the Neolithic Age, exquisite artifacts, such as jade cong, jade bi disk and jade zhang blade, have already appeared in the archaeological ruins of Liangzhu City, which is located at the lower reaches of the Yangtze River in Jiangsu and Zhejiang provinces. Being a master of the skill needed to collect and carve jade objects early, the Ancient Shu people, who lived in the upper reaches of the Yangtze River in the Sichuan Basin, also showed their interest in jade objects. Jade was used as an ornament by them. They were also keen to make jade sacrificial vessels and used them in the sacrificial activities which were frequently held. At the Jinsha site, however, there are more jade artifacts with varied types and exquisite shapes, which never fail to impress.

According to archaeologists, the quantity of jade artifacts excavated at the Jinsha site is very large and accounts for 40% of the total number of excavated artifacts. These jade artifacts are various in types and shapes, including jade

FAR LEFT *Four-node jade cong from the Jinsha site*

LEFT *Collared bulged jade bi from the Jinsha site*

Flat jade cong from the Jinsha site

cong, jade zhang blade, jade bi, jade ring, jade ax, jade adze, jade knife, jade sword, jade dagger-ax, jade tablet, jade seashell-shape pendant, and jade figure, as well as animal and plant-shaped jade ornaments. Most of these artifacts were made of tremolite jade, which were excellent in material selection. With the technique of cutting, chiseling, polishing, drilling, and carving, these jade artifacts showed a fairly high level of processing technology and were also distinctive in shape, ornamentation, and cultural connotation.

Mostly, these jade wares were used as sacrificial utensils in sacrificial ceremonies in Ancient Shu. In addition, there were also 200 pieces of bead, pipe, and flake shaped turquoises, as well as several agate beads, which may have been ornaments for the Ancient Shu people. The jade wares at the Jinsha site made it possible for us to learn more about the Ancient Shu, to peek into the kingdom and its people's life, experiencing their sacrificial activities, religious faiths, spiritual beliefs, aesthetic tastes, and local customs. While most of these jade wares manifested strong regional cultural characteristics of Ancient Shu, some of them reflected the influence of other cultures, revealing the communication and connection between the Ancient Shu civilization and other regional civilizations.

Among the numerous jade artifacts unearthed at the Jinsha site, the most impressive one is jade cong. We know that the jade cong has been known for a long time. Since ancient times, it has been used as an important ritual vessel to worship heaven, mountains, and rivers. It was also used by the ancient kings when they dispatched envoys to visit other countries. In addition, it was often used for funeral rites, as detailed in the *Rites of Zhou* and other ancient texts. Archaeological findings tell us that the cong was an artifact typical of the Liangzhu Culture, which was popular in southeast China about 5,000 years ago. It was also found in some Neolithic sites in the middle and lower reaches of the Yangtze River and the Longshan Culture (3000–1900 BC) site in the middle and lower reaches of the Yellow River. Being more popular in the Xia, Shang, and Zhou dynasties, jade cong were widely unearthed in the ruins and tombs of the period in Henan, Shandong, Sichuan, and other places. For example, one piece of broken jade cong was unearthed at the Erlitou site in Yanshi, Henan Province, and 14 pieces of jade cong were discovered at the Fuhao tomb at the Yin Ruins in Anyang, Henan Province. Meanwhile, at Dayangzhou, Xingan County, Jiangxi Province, one piece of jade cong was excavated from the Shang tomb. What's more, jade congs were found at the Sanxingdui site in Guanghan, Sichuan Province as well. In addition, there are also numerous heirlooms, with as many as 31 jade congs recorded in the *Textual Research of Ancient Jade with Illustrations* written by Wu Daheng in the Qing Dynasty (AD 1636–1912). More than ten pieces of jade congs have been unearthed at the Jinsha site, which is a considerable number. It has fully demonstrated the appreciation and fondness of the rulers of the Jinsha site for the jade congs, a special ceremonial object. Among the ten pieces of jade congs, there are both jade congs from Liangzhu Culture with exquisite types and shapes and jade congs that enjoy a change in style on the basis of the characteristics of jade congs from Liangzhu Culture. Analysis of their features and styles suggests that some of them had a long history and may be heirlooms, some may come from the southeast region of the middle and lower reaches of the Yangtze River, and some may be sacrificial objects made by local jade craftsmen.

Let's begin with the jade cong unearthed at the Jinsha site, which is 22.26 cm high and weighs 1,358 g. This cuboid was made of translucent green jade. Through professional accreditation, the main composition of this cuboid is tremolite nephrite. Enjoying a white calcific surface with some striped light-black spots, it is round inside and square outside. The profile is a rectangular prism with a larger upper part than a lower part. With a hole drilled from both ends of the cuboid, there are two convex circular orifices at its upper and lower ends.

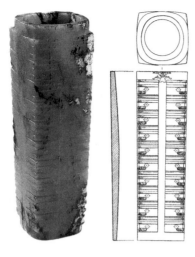

The long grey jade cong from the Jinsha site and its line drawing

On the wall of this cuboid, there are vertical grooves in the middle of the four sides, dividing each side of its body into left and right parts. There are also nine small horizontal grooves on the wall to divide its body into 10 nodes, forming altogether 80 convex surfaces on this jade cong. On every corner of the nodes is a simplified god face. There are altogether 40 faces on the cuboid. The surface and hole wall of the jade cong is carefully ground and polished. Some shallow carved lines are now blurred, which indicates that this object has been used for a long time. Archaeologists introduced the concept that the specific features of each god-face pattern can be roughly divided into four layers from top to bottom. In its design, parallel lines are used to represent the feather crown of the god; the eyes and eyeballs of the god are represented by circles, large or small, carved on the wall of the object; and at the same time, the mouth of the god is in place of some geometric patterns. Formed by various carving patterns, all these 40 god-face patterns are full of mysterious messages, making this jade cong exceptionally exquisite and marvelous.

An incised god-man pattern, it should be noted, was carved at the upper orifices of this cuboid. Standing with stout, short feet, the god has a strong body, which is smoothly shaped. With a miraculous crown on his head, he raised his long arms horizontally to both sides. Both ends of the arms are carved with long, flowing sleeves and curled feathers, making his arms the wings of a bird. As a combination of freehand and abstract, the whole image is full of fun with a rich symbolic meaning. Especially, the stretching and flowing body and the strange patterns of long sleeves and feather crown could easily bring a rich imagination to people, giving them a magical sense of feeling free to travel between heaven and earth. However, these carved lines are so blurred that careful observation should be made from a certain angle to see them clearly. Through comparative study, it is found that most of the patterns on the long cuboids unearthed at the archaeological ruins of

Jade tablet with bas-relief pattern of insect from the Jinsha site   *Battle-ax with an animal-face pattern from the Jinsha site*

Liangzhu Culture are carved at their upper orifices; and this long jade cong discovered at Jinsha site is identical to the jade congs of the Liangzhu Culture. Since it was unearthed at the Jinsha site, it has received broad attention from the academic community. Many scholars have carefully observed this cuboid with profound interest, believing it a state-level treasure among all unearthed artifacts of the same kind. As for the god-man pattern on the cuboid, some scholars speculated that it should be a crown-shaped symbol. With flying feathers on both sides of the crown, the whole pattern may be a hieroglyphic of "emperor" in ancient books. Thus, it can be concluded that these patterns are a symbol of great power, and cuboids carved with this image should be used by the ruling class. The image symbol also tells us that the jade cong unearthed at the Jinsha site may not have been made by local jade craftsmen, for it was obviously made much earlier than other artifacts unearthed at the same time. Therefore, there is speculation that this cuboid should be a relic in the Ancient Shu, which may come from the Liangzhu cultural area in the middle and lower reaches of the Yangtze River, and it became a special ritual instrument used by the ruling class of the Ancient Shu in the Shang and Zhou dynasties in sacrificial activities. It was common for the Ancient Shu people to keep and use important ritual vessels of previous dynasties, for they had a tradition of cherishing heirloom jade. Thus, in archaeological excavation, the artifacts of previous dynasties could always be found at the sites or tombs of later generations.

Incidentally, among the numerous jade congs unearthed at the archaeological ruins of Liangzhu Culture, there were also some god-man patterns and animal-face patterns carved in shallow relief. They were more exquisite and complex, and their connotations were richer. For example,

Jade cong from the Liangzhu culture

the relief of the "animal-faced god-man pattern" on the large jade cong unearthed in the tomb of the Liangzhu Culture site in Fanshan, Yuhang District, Zhejiang Province, showed the rich imagination of the Ancient Shu people to worship heaven and arth and the symbolic meaning of the interaction between human and god. The upper part of the pattern was a godlike man wearing a feather crown, and the lower part was a mythical beast with round and wide-open eyes. In addition, at the two sides of the patterns, some deformed bird images are portrayed with artistic exaggeration. Meanwhile, with his arms held out flat, the man bends his hands downward to control the beast behind him, which vividly visualizes the view of riding a mythical beast to access heaven.

Similar patterns can also be seen on the battle-ax unearthed in the tomb of the Liangzhu Culture site. The jade battle-ax, a ceremonial vessel similar to a scepter, was often used as a symbol of the possession of military command in ancient times. For example, in the *Records of the Grand Historian · Yin Dynasty*, there is a record that "With an ax on his hands, Tang quelled the rebellion of Kunwu tribe," and in the *Book of Documents · Speech at Muye*, it is recorded that emperor Wu led his troops with a golden ax in his left hand and a military flag in his right hand. The carving of the typical pattern of jade cong on jade battle-ax also fully illustrated the extraordinary symbolic meaning of the pattern. Some scholars believe that such reliefs on jade cong and jade battle-ax may be tribal symbols, divine badges worshipped by Liangzhu people, or totems adored by primitive nations. It is known that the belief in heaven and earth worship and the close relationship between gods and men took strong roots in the minds of the ancient people. In this view, mythical beasts served as assistants of wizards, who acted as mediators between human beings and gods. Obviously, the animal-faced pattern on the jade cong of the Liangzhu Culture site was related to this concept. As such, the god-man pattern on the long jade cong from the Jinsha site may be endowed with a similar meaning as well. It should be noted that patterns on the jade congs from the Liangzhu Culture site were related to the time of popularity, which could be divided into three stages: in the early stage, most of them were animal-faced patterns; in the middle stage, there were patterns featuring a mix of animal face and human face; and in the late stage, the majority of patterns were human-faced patterns. Despite there being some changes with time, the symbolic meanings of animal faces and human faces remained the same.

According to the *Rites of Zhou · Officers of Spring*, "the six vessels made of jade were offered to the four directions of heaven and earth, with a gray disk ritualizing the sky and yellow cuboid ritualizing the earth"; the jade cong was used to ritualize the earth as a sacrificial vessel. However, this statement was mysterious, as well as overly general and simplistic.

Research by contemporary scholars has revealed that, in fact, the connotations and meanings of jade congs are exceptionally rich. To sum up, it is mainly reflected in the following aspects. First of all, it symbolizes the belief that heaven is round and earth square. The jade cong is square inside and round outside, which makes it a symbol of the link between heaven and earth. As a magic tool that connects human beings and gods, it has been used in sacrificial activities. Second, there is a close relationship between jade congs and wizards, who "used jade to serve the gods," as not only were the figures of the gods or wizards engraved in the patterns, but also the jade cong itself was a magic tool used by the wizard. Since wizards were a special class who wielded divine power in ancient times, jade objects used by them were also often seen as the symbol of divine power. Moreover, being used as a symbol of status and wealth for rulers or the noble class, jade congs were mostly buried in tombs as burial goods after the death of the user, which is a relatively common phenomenon in the tombs of the Liangzhu Culture site and the Yin-Shang Dynasty. It can be seen from all these facts that jade congs were widely used, and being a special ritual vessel used in sacrificial activities was one of their most important functions.

It is known, in the minds of the Ancient Shu people, there is a close relationship between man and gods. Containing the imagination of connecting heaven and earth, the bronze sacred tree and bronze statues of witches doing sacrificial activities unearthed from Sanxingdui site vividly demonstrated this view, except that there is also the custom and tradition of worshipping birds and witches for the people in the Ancient Shu and

Liangzhu. Both of them advocated the role of divine power in social life, with witches as the leaders of their clans or tribes. It is precisely because the early Shu culture and Liangzhu Culture have so much in common, that the Ancient Shu people could easily resonate with jade congs from Liangzhu Culture. They not only accepted this typical Liangzhu cultural artifact but also started to imitate and occupy jade congs in the Ancient Shu ritual activities for a long time. What should be noted is that the Yin people, who also accepted jade congs, mainly used them for "jade funerals," while the jade congs excavated at the Sanxingdui and Jinsha sites had nothing to do with burials (they were not excavated in tombs), which not only shows that the Ancient Shu people treasured jade congs but also shows the difference of using jade objects between the Shu and Yin peoples.

The information disclosed by the jade cong from the Jinsha site is extremely rich. What it told us is not only the wonderful implication, rich connotation, long history, and great influence of the jade cong, but also the long-standing cultural and economic exchanges between ancient regional civilizations. Academics generally believe that the Ancient Shu people's communication with the Central Plains and its surrounding areas may have two ways, water, and land. Among them, the main route was shipping along the Yangtze River. Although the exact time of their mutual exchanges remains a mystery, it is clear that it may have started from antiquity for the Ancient Shu people and Liangzhu people, who lived in the middle and lower reaches of the Yangtze River, had exchanges and cultural transmission as early as the Shang and Zhou dynasties. To be a handed-down ritual vessel in Jinsha site, the long jade cong is a typical jade object of Liangzhu Culture, which probably entered Sichuan through the middle reaches of the Yangtze River. Four thousand years ago, both sides of the Yangtze River were covered in lush green vegetation and forests. Its surpassed ecological environment and the convenience of shipping up and down the river may be far better than we thought. With the development of human civilization, such mutual cultural and economic exchanges had been increasing and had become more frequent in the Shang and Zhou dynasties. All these interactions and mutual influences are reflected in the patterns of unearthed objects. For example, jade articles of the Liangzhu Culture were carved with typical animal-face patterns, a combination of the characteristics of humans and animals, and they adopted crown-shaped patterns. Similar patterns could be

Phoenix-shaped dagger-ax from Yuyao, Hemudu, Zhejiang Province

found on objects excavated from the Sanxingdui site and the Jinsha site as well, such as the bronze animal-face object in Sanxingdui site and the jade human head in Jinsha site. For another example, both people worshipped birds and the sun. In the Hemudu cultural site in Yuyao, Zhejiang Province, an ivory carving of "two phoenixes rising sun" and a bone dagger of "two birds carrying the sun" were unearthed. The pottery and jade objects of the Liangzhu Culture site enjoy evolved bird patterns as well. In the artifacts unearthed at the Sanxingdui site and Jinsha site, the concept of worshipping the bird and sun is made with a lot of innovation and incisive expression.

The jade cong unearthed from the Jinsha site also shows that the learning of foreign cultures did not weaken the Ancient Shu people's personality and distinctive characteristics but made them more energetic through inclusive absorption. The intelligent and open-minded Ancient Shu people often imitated and gave full play to their innovations as they absorbed and accepted foreign cultural elements. Being an imitation of the handed-down jade cong of Liangzhu Culture, the yellow jade cong unearthed from the Jinsha site enjoys a more concise style. The Ancient Shu people also imitated some jade objects from the Central Plains, such as jade daggers-ax, jade swords, collared bulged bi, and jade zhang blade, etc. It can be seen that these jade objects are similar in shape to the jade artifacts from Yin-Shang Dynasty, but also enjoy an evolution of style and distinguishing features. The same situation has already appeared on the Sanxingdui site. For example, the bronze plate inlaid with turquoise unearthed from Sanxingdui site is very similar to the bronze plate unearthed at the Erlitou site in Henan Province in shape, but they have differences in patterns and styles as well. This phenomenon is obviously the result of imitation through cultural exchanges between the two places, except that, the bronze statues and bronze Lei unearthed at the Sanxingdui site also show the imitation of ritual vessels in the Central Plains by the Ancient Shu people. The jade oval-shaped artifact unearthed at the

Jade oval-shaped artifact from the Jinsha site   *Bronze tablet from the Sanxingdui site*

Jinsha site is worth mentioning, as it may be a specially made jade object that imitates the bronze tablets of the Erlitou and Sanxingdui sites in size and shape. It is because of this exchange and innovation that the Ancient Shu culture was more colorful, and the Ancient Shu society during the Shang and Zhou dynasties was thriving and flourishing.

10

———◇◇◇◇◇◇———

Splendid Culture and Prosperity of the Ancient Capital of Shu

When, for various reasons, the Sanxingdui site declined, the Jinsha site took its place and completed its evolution from a large settlement to a kingdom capital.

The archaeological discoveries suggest that the Jinsha site was a major settlement of the Ancient Shu people during the Shang and Zhou dynasties or a very prosperous urban center. There is little dispute about that. As early as when Sanxingdui was the capital of the prosperous Ancient Shu Kingdom, Jinsha had already been the habitat of some clans and tribes of the Ancient Shu ethnic group. Among them, there might be clans that worshipped birds and fish and tribes that took stone tigers and golden frogs as symbols of worship. They all had a strong sense of sun worship and followed the tradition of holding sacrificial activities frequently. Their growth and prosperity might result from marriage or alliance with each other. When Sanxingdui declined due to various reasons, Jinsha played a role in its place, and finally completed the process of development and evolution from a large settlement to a kingdom's capital.

The Ancient Shu, who settled at the Jinsha site, probably started with a small population, and their tribes were relatively weak at first. In terms of both divine and royal authority, they were subject to the rule of Sanxingdui, the capital of the kingdom, which co-dominated the political order with Jinsha. By the time of the Shang and Zhou dynasties, the Ancient Shu clan at the Jinsha site had already been very strong. Although their sacrificial utensils were still of a lower grade and specification, it was indisputable that they had made great progress in all aspects.

Archaeological excavations revealed that Jinsha had been fairly prosperous at that time. A ruling class composed of clan witches and tribal leaders was formed. Large-scale sacrificial ceremonies were often held. There was a clear division of labor in various trades, and the production of pottery and jade, as well as the processing of gold, reached a very high level. Rice-based agricultural production was greatly developed. Animal husbandry and hunting also reached a considerable scale. At that time, the population of the Jinsha site (including the Twelve Bridges site and the surrounding area) greatly increased, and the whole society was greatly enriched from the material to the spiritual. Jinsha showed a trend of growing prosperity, Whether in terms of the scale of the site or the development of its culture. The latecomer gained the upper hand over the early starter.

We know that the prosperity of a nation and an era is always inseparable from economic strength. This was the case with the Ancient Shu Kingdom of the Sanxingdui period, and the rise of the Jinsha site was no exception. The Ancient Shu Kingdom, with Chengdu Plain as its center, was blessed with natural resources, as stated in ancient documents such as the *Classic of Mountains and Seas*, *History of Kings of the Shu*, and *Record of the Huayang Kingdom*. The field of Duguang had advantageous natural resources. "Corps like soybean, rice, and wheat, grew naturally and ripened twice a year. In Ancient Shu Kingdom, there were lush mountains and lucid waters, and fruits ripened successively during seasons." "It's also rich in rare metals such as gold, silver, iron, lead, and tin. Mineral resources were also abundant, like jade, sapphire, chalk, and ocher. Brocade, embroidery, ivory, felt, rhino horns, and linen gave a picture of handicraft industry." "In addition, the Ancient Shu Kingdom had a vast territory, extended from Baoxie in the north to Xiong'er and Lingguan in the south. Shu Kingdom took Mount. Yulei and Emei as the citadel. Jiang, Qian, Mian, and Luo within were rivers and lakes. The Shu people raised poultry in Wen Shan and farmed in the Nanzhong area." These accounts painted a picture of what a thriving and prosperous society it was.

Jade human head from the Jinsha site

Although there were many words of praise, the information disclosed was quite authentic.

From the information provided by archaeological findings, it is clear that the Ancient Shu formed stable farming settlements very early and then early cities emerged. During the Shang and Zhou dynasties, the Ancient Shu Kingdom developed on a considerable scale in terms of agriculture, animal husbandry, secondary industries, and handicrafts. In addition, fishing and hunting activities and trade with the outside were also prosperous. All these set the economy of the Ancient Shu Kingdom on a firm foundation and formed a splendid inland agricultural civilization. The Ancient Shu had a long history of rice cultivation, and by the time of the Qin Dynasty's annexation of Ba Shu, the Shu Kingdom had become a center of rice production in the upper reaches of the Yangtze River. At the Jinsha site during the Shang and Zhou dynasties, it was clear that rice farming was also the mainstay with considerable yield. In addition to daily consumption, the surplus was used for wine making and storage. This is confirmed by a large number of potteries unearthed at the Jinsha site, which was closely related to the diet of the Ancient Shu people. These potteries were used for many purposes, cooking, eating, drinking, or storing, reflecting the diversity of food and the abundance of agricultural products at that time. There were also rows of cellars for storage. The ceramic industry boomed as a result of agricultural prosperity and daily consumption. A number of kiln sites have been found at the Jinsha site, 17 of which were at the "Sanhe Garden" of Huangzhong Village, indicating the scale of the pottery industry at that time.

Plenty of artifacts unearthed at the Jinsha site gave a booming scene of handicrafts and agricultural and sideline industry at that time. There were specialized practitioners in bronze casting, and gold and jade ware production, which was particularly developed. The excavated artifacts show that bronze statues and diverse gold and jade wares were made to meet the demands of sacrificial and ritual activities that were frequently held. The importance of rituals in social life of the Ancient Shu led the ruling class, who wielded

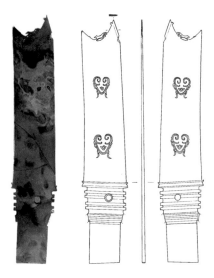

Jade zhang blade from the Jinsha site and its line drawings

divine power, to use all their valuable resources to the best. It also led the producers to give full play to their imagination and creativity in the variety of shapes and craftsmanship, thus contributing to the prosperity of the industry.

The jade wares unearthed at the Jinsha site are not only large in quantity but also rich in variety. Most of them are "jade for rituals," while some may have multiple functions, such as jade ring, jade bi, jade cong, and jade tablet, which served as both ritual wares and decorations. Other examples are jade dagger-ax, jade sword, and jade spear, which may have been both guards of honor and have practical uses. There are also jade axes, jade adzes, and jade chisels, etc., which can be used as both sacrificial offerings and tools.

It shows a high level of production technique, whether it is the selection of jade materials, cutting or carving, drilling, or polishing. Great carving skills can be seen through the animal shapes and patterns on the wares. Many of these elaborate jade artifacts are among the finest artifacts of the Shang and Zhou dynasties. In particular, the figures and animals are masterpieces of jade carving. A large number of craftsmen and a strong labor force were required in the production of so many jade wares, which revealed the prosperity of the jade industry at that time.

The numerous gold products unearthed at the Jinsha site suggest that gold processing also flourished at that time. Lots of laborers engaged in this industry from mining to smelting. According to the information released so far, there are as many as 31 relatively complete gold artifacts unearthed at the Jinsha site. These gold objects come in a variety of forms, ranging from gold masks to gold crown belts, and are exquisitely crafted and of a high level. Some goldware and gold jewelry are endowed with rich symbolic meaning by ingenious and imaginative patterns engraved on them. For example, the exquisite Sun and Immortal Birds Gold Ornament is a rare masterpiece of

Trumpet-shaped gold object from the
Jinsha site

Gold mask from the tomb of Mycenae
in Greece

Bronze mask from Sanxingdui pit No. 1

Gold mask from the Jinsha site

gold in the Shang and Zhou periods. The magic patterns on the gold crown belt and the unique form of the gold frog decoration are also classic works in the gold processing technology of 3,000 years ago. The artistic charm of these ingenious gold objects is still amazing today.

Sanxingdui site also unearthed a large number of gold ware, such as gold staffs, gold masks, gold animal figures, and ornaments, all of which were unique, demonstrating high processing and production skills and rich cultural connotations. The goldware unearthed at the Jinsha site further revealed the extraordinary achievements of the Ancient Shu in gold mining and processing.

In terms of style and cultural connotation, the gold artifacts excavated at the Jinsha site are the same as those at the Sanxingdui site, but they are more innovative in technology and patterns. According to the history of world archaeology, in the 1870s, a large number of gold objects were unearthed in Mycenaean tombs in ancient Greece. In the 1920s, more than 1,700 gold objects, such as human-like golden coffins and golden masks, were unearthed in Tutankhamun's tomb during the New Kingdom period of ancient Egypt, which are recognized by some scholars as masterpieces of Bronze Age civilization in Central Asia and the West.

The archaeological excavation at the two sites confirmed that the Ancient Shu people were also one of the earliest ancient tribes in the world to mine and use gold, which corrected the bias in Western art history and enriched the history of world art. The excavations show that the Ancient Shu people were skilled in processing gold during the Shang and Zhou dynasties, and the gold masks, gold staffs, gold crown belts, as well as the Sun and Immortal Birds Gold Ornament they made were as exquisite as those of ancient Egyptian and Greek civilizations.

Archaeological discoveries at the Jinsha site also suggest that the Ancient Shu had flourishing agricultural and sideline industries during the Shang and Zhou periods, with livestock breeding and animal husbandry likely to have been more developed. Most animal bones excavated from Sanxingdui pit No. 1 were identified as medium-sized animals, such as pigs and sheep, and a few were large animals, such as buffaloes. Five bronze buffalo heads and a bronze rooster were excavated from Sanxingdui pit No. 2, while a number of bronze zun and bronze earthenware jars were cast with three bull heads, three sheep heads, or four sheep heads on their shoulders, respectively. The Jinsha site also unearthed a number of copper bull heads. These archaeological finds are obviously evidence of the large number of domestic animals kept by the Shu people in ancient times. With reference to a large number of livestock kept in the ancient city of Sanxingdui, it is assumed that a similar number of livestock would have been kept in the large settlement at the Jinsha site. In addition, the Ancient Shu was active in fishing and hunting. As an important supplement to their agricultural industry, it was a further source of food. The abundance of hunted material at the time is reflected in the large quantities of wild boar tusks, and antlers excavated at the Jinsha site.

Archaeological excavations have revealed that the construction industry of the Ancient Shu was also well-developed during the Shang and Zhou periods. A large number of houses have been found at Sanxingdui, and many building remains have been discovered at the Jinsha site, most of which are of wood (bamboo) and mud construction which was popular in the Ancient

Bronze chicken from the   *Bronze buffalo head from*   *Bronze bull head from the*
Sanxingdui pit No. 1   *the Sanxingdui pit No. 2*   *Jinsha site*

Shu. The large buildings were probably owned by the princes and ruling classes, while the smaller houses were probably the residence of the civilian class. In terms of construction methods, both the larger buildings and the smaller houses had foundation trenches and dense small column holes. The larger buildings had large post holes at regular intervals (around 1 m), a remnant of large beams used in their construction at the time. This building remains at the Jinsha site basically faced southeast, which was presumed to be related to the sense of orientation of the Ancient Shu. It suggested that the Ancient Shu had learned to make plans when they were building. At the Shierqiao site, which is slightly later than the Jinsha site, a large area of timber-framed buildings was excavated. It can be seen that the buildings were of Ganlan style, typical of the southern region. They are closely related to the natural environment of the Chengdu Plain, with its abundant rainfall and wet ground. The buildings at the Jinsha site, built along the river, belonged to the same cultural type as the Shierqiao site and were probably also of Ganlan style. Their destruction and obliteration were also due to flooding. In general, the architectural style of the Ancient Shu is a true reflection of the social life at that time, because it included both the large buildings pursued by the ruling class and small houses which represented the lifestyle of the civilian class.

The sacrificial activities of the Ancient Shu Kingdom during the Shang and Zhou dynasties were also very prosperous, as artifacts from the Sanxingdui and Jinsha sites have revealed. In addition to the worship of the sun god, the sun, and the rain, which have been introduced earlier, the frequent sacrifices at the Jinsha site may also include those to heaven and earth, to the god of

Bronze dragon and tiger zun from
Sanxingdui pit No. 1

Bronze lei from Sanxingdui pit No. 2

land, to sacred mountains, to ancestors, and to ghosts and gods, divination, praying for a high yield, the worship of totems, and the worship of nature, as well as exorcism activities of witchcraft and driving away evil spirits. It is assumed from the functional layout of the large settlement at the Jinsha site that there may have been clan temples or shrines dedicated to sacrifice rituals and possibly multiple fixed ritual sites. The scale of their rituals may also have been varied, ranging from large-scale rituals to seasonal rituals, and possibly rituals for special circumstances. The sacrificial activities are likely to be closely related to the social life of the Ancient Shu. The bronze standing figure as an envoy of the sun god and the stone kneeling figure used for "praying for rain" were both used in the hope of gaining the protection of the sun god and of bringing a good harvest to agriculture through sacrifices. The second was to offer sacrifices to heaven and earth, mountains, and rivers. A large number of ceremonial jades unearthed at the Jinsha site are related to such sacrificial activities. The third was to sacrifice ancestors, ghosts, and gods. The small jade figure and jade ax with an animal-faced pattern excavated at the Jinsha site are likely to have been used by the Ancient Shu in such sacrificial activities. Of particular note is the fact that the concept of "Returning to Heaven" was once a theme of the Ancient Shu and widespread in the Bashu area, which is closely related to such sacrificial activities and the unique funeral customs of Ancient Shu. Worship of the god of land is likely to be a frequent sacrifice held at that time, and a large number of wild boar fangs and antlers, the blood of slaughtered animals, and fine wine may be sacrifices in such type of sacrifice. In addition, sacrificial exorcism may have been a common part of the Ancient Shu's social life, associated with the expulsion of evil spirits, witchcraft, and funeral rituals. Most of these sacrificial activities are related to witchcraft, which not only shows the special status of witches in the Ancient Shu Kingdom but also reflects the prosperity of witchcraft at that time. When the Ancient Shu held sacrificial activities, there would be corresponding sacrificial ceremonies and probably sacrificial dances. The *Classic of Mountains and Seas · Zhongshan Sutra* reveals that the ancient tribes in the Minshan region were known to have practiced ritual dances, as revealed in the *Classic of Mountains and Seas · Zhongshan Sutra*. Up to now, we can still see the influence of such customs in some minority-inhabited areas in the southwest.

The archaeological discoveries at the Sanxingdui and Jinsha sites also show that the Ancient Shu were not isolated from the rest of the world though they were in an inland area. They were adept at pioneering and innovating and had cultural and economic exchanges with the middle and lower reaches of the Yangtze River, the Central Plains and northwest regions of the Yellow River Basin, the vast southwest Yi region, and even South and Central Asia at that time. It was through exchanges with the outside world that the clever Shu people learned and absorbed foreign cultural elements, which contributed to the prosperity of inland agricultural civilization and the flourishing of Ancient Shu society.

In addition to cultural interaction, this long-term exchange between the Ancient Shu and the surrounding areas also promoted the flow and migration of population, which played an important role in the development of the Ancient Shu civilization. In the history of Ancient Shu, Shushan, and Chancong were ancient tribes that rose in the upper reaches of the Min River and later followed the Min River out of the mountains into the Chengdu Plain, becoming the founder of the Ancient Shu Kingdom. The subsequent Yufu, Duyu, and Kaiming were not indigenous folks in the Ancient Shu Kingdom. These foreign tribes or clans that became the rulers of the Ancient Shu not only contributed to the rise and fall of the Ancient Shu, but also added to the richness of the splendid Ancient Shu civilization. The Ancient Shu also moved and migrated to other places. After Duyu lost his country, he may have fled to Liangshan and Yunnan with his followers. It is said that the

Yi people are the descendants of Duyu. King Anyang, the last prince of the Kaiming Dynasty, also moved away from his native land after the country was broken, leading tens of thousands of people to the land of Jiaotong, where he reigned for more than 100 years. It is these events in history that made the Ancient Shu Kingdom a civilization center in the southwest region of the upper reaches of the Yangtze River. At the same time, it expanded the spread of the Ancient Shu civilization, which had a positive and extensive influence on the surrounding regions.

All in all, the archaeological discoveries at the Jinsha site show us the colorful social life and spiritual outlook of the Ancient Shu people. As a large settlement in the Chengdu area during the Shang and Zhou dynasties, the splendid remains of the Jinsha site thousands of years ago are now a dazzling pearl that reveals the roots of Chengdu, a famous historical and cultural city in the west. The ingenuity and creations of the Ancient Shu people are full of eternal charm which not only makes us gasp in admiration but also writes a brilliant chapter in the history of Chinese civilization.

Postscript

It is indeed a very good idea to examine and promote the long and splendid history and culture of Chengdu from different perspectives through a series of books. With the rapid development of the western region and economic construction, Chengdu, as a metropolis, is undergoing rapid changes, with old neighborhoods fading away and traditional folkways and customs being replaced by new ones. However, its history and culture should not be forgotten, as they are the roots of the famous Western city, and the charm of the Land of Abundance.

Jinsha archaeology is indeed a topic well worth writing about. I can still remember the scene when I heard the news of the discovery of the Jinsha site in the spring of 2001. The literary and academic fraternity rushed to tell each other about it, and their excitement and surprise were indescribable. For scholars with a deep affinity for studying the Ancient Shu civilization, the large amount of archaeological data provided by the Jinsha site was very important. Whether it is to reveal the historical and cultural development of Ancient Shu, or to understand the rise of Chengdu's "mother city," the archaeology of Jinsha is of great importance. The Chengdu archaeological team, which was in charge of the excavations at the Jinsha site, was a pioneering team: small in number, but all in their prime. What is admirable is not only their work progress but also their openness and willingness to regard academia as a public instrument for the world. With the support of Mr. Wang Yi and other colleagues and friends, I conducted some research on the Jinsha site using published materials and was one of the first authors to write a book on my experiences. Many of my academic insights were written in the book *Jinsha in Ancient Shu—An Exploration of the Jinsha Site and Ancient Shu Civilization.* The writing of this book, *Archaeology of Jinsha,* gave me another opportunity to explore and reflect. In accordance with the requirements of book planning, this book adopts a more popular and fluent narrative, and it ensures academic and cultural tastes at the same time. Due to space limitations, everything from the introduction of archaeological finds to the appreciation of excavated artifacts can only be condensed into a limited number of chapters. However, I believe that the brevity of the text and the benefit of the illustrations will provide the reader with the most convenient reading, which also shows the charm and characteristics of this series.

As a writer who has been writing literature and history for many years, I would like to thank all those who have cared for and supported me as my new book is about to come out. I also hope that readers will well receive the book.

The above is the postscript written after the book was published in October 2005. From the information gathered since then, the book was well received in the book market, not being overwhelmed by the vast sea of other books, and it quickly went out of print.

Recently, thanks to the favor of the publisher, this book is going to be reprinted. It is with the same sincerity that I would like to thank all my friends who have supported me over the years, and most of all, I would like to thank my enthusiastic readers, and I hope that this book will become your favorite reading material, which will be my greatest gratification.

Mid-Autumn, 2021
At Gengyuzhai in Chengdu

References

Archaeology of Chengdu. *Chengdu Archaeological Discoveries (2001)*. Beijing: China's Science Publishing & Media Ltd, 2003.

———. *Chengdu Archaeological Discoveries (2002)*. Beijing: China's Science Publishing & Media Ltd, 2004.

———. *Jinsha Village Site—Reproduce the Glorious Ancient Capital of Shu*. Chengdu: Sichuan People's Publishing House, 2005.

Archaeology of Chengdu and School of Archaeology, and Museology of Peking University. *Treasure Hunting in Jinsha—Cultural Relics Unearthed at Jinsha Village Site*. Beijing: Cultural Relics Press, 2002.

Cao Xuequan. *Records of Scenic Spots in Sichuan*. Chongqing: Chongqing Publishing Group, 1984.

Chang Qu. *A Correction and Completion with Pictographic Annotation for Chronicles of Huayang*. Edited by Liu Lin. Chengdu: Sichuan Classics Publishing House, 1984.

———. *A Correction and Completion with Pictographic Annotation for Chronicles of Huayang*. Edited by Ren Naiqiang. Shanghai: Shanghai Ancient Books Publishing House, 1987.

Du You. *Tong Dian*. Beijing: Zhonghua Book Company, 1988.

Shanghai Classics Publishing House. *Twenty-Two Philosophers*. Shanghai: Shanghai Classics Publishing House, 1986.

Hu Houxuan. *Excavations in the Yin Sites*. Beijing: Learning Life Publishing House, 1995.

Li Fang. *Imperial Readings of the Taiping Era*. Beijing: Zhonghua Book Company, 1960.

Li Ji. *An Yang*. Shijiazhuang: Hebei Education Press, 2000.

Li Shaoming. *The Research of Culture of the Xia Dynasty under the Reign of Yu*. Chengdu: Sichuan Classics Publishing House, 2000.

Lu liancheng, and Hu Zhisheng. *Yu State cemeteries in Baoji*. Beijing: Cultural Relics Press, 1988.

Lu Sixian. *Mythology Archaeology*. Beijing: Cultural Relics Press, 1995.

Meng Wentong. *Research on Ba-Shu History*. Chengdu: Sichuan People's Publishing House, 1981.

———. *The Collected Works of Meng Wentong*. Vol. 2. Chengdu: Sichuan Classics Publishing House, 1993.

Ouyang Xun. *Arts Class Together*. Shanghai: Shanghai Ancient Books Publishing House, 1982.

RuanYuan. *Thirteen Classics*. Beijing: Zhonghua Book Company, 1980.

Rui Chuanming, and Yu Taishan. *Comparison of Chinese and Western Decorative Patterns*. Shanghai: Shanghai Classics Publishing House, 1995.

Sichuan Institute of Cultural Relics and Archaeology. *Sanxingdui Sacrificial Pit*. Beijing: Cultural Relics Press, 1999.

Song Zhenhao. *Social Life History of Xia and Shang Dynasties*. Beijing: China Social Sciences Press, 1994.

Song Zhaolin. *Witch and Witchcraft*. Chengdu: Sichuan Ethnic Publishing House, 1989.

Tan Jihe. *The Critical Notes on Ba-Shu Culture*. Chengdu: Sichuan people's publishing house, 2004.

The Institute of Archaeology. *Chinese Academy of Social Sciences, Archaeological Excavation and Researches in the Yin Ruins*. Beijing: China's Science Publishing & Media Ltd, 1984.

Tong Enzheng. *Ancient Ba-Shu*. Chengdu: Sichuan People's Publishing House, 1979.

———. *The Collected Works of Tong Enzheng*. Chongqin: Chongqin Publishing Group, 1998.

Xiao Bing. *Cultural Interpretation of Songs of Chu*. Changsha: Hubei People's Publishing Press, 1991.

Xu Zhongshu. *Selected History Papers of Xu Zhongshu*. Beijing: Zhonghua Book Company, 1998.

Yan kejun. *The Whole Ancient Three Dynasties, Qin, Han, Three Kingdoms, and Six Dynasties*. Beijing: Zhonghua Book Company, 1958.

Ye Shuxian. *Chinese Mythological Philosophy*. Beijing: China's Social Sciences Press, 1992.

Yuan Ke. *The Classic of Mountains and Seas: A Collation and Annotation*. Chengdu: Sichuan Classics Publishing House, 1993.

Zhang Zhengming. *Chu Cultural History*. Shanghai: Shanghai People's Publishing House, 1987.

Zhejiang Classics Publishing House. *One Hundred Philosophers' Writings*. Hangzhou: Zhejiang Classics Publishing House, 1998.

Zheng Dekun. *Sichuan Ancient History*. Chengdu: Huaxi University Museum, 1946.

Zhu Boxiong. *World Art History*. Jinan: Shandong Fine Arts Publishing House, 1989.

Zhu Di. *The Research on Primitive Culture*. Beijing: Joint Publishing House, 1988.

ABOUT THE AUTHOR

HUANG JIANHUA is a researcher at the Sichuan Provincial Institute of Cultural Relics and Archaeology, a member of the Chinese Writers Association, and a special librarian at the Research Institute of Culture and History of Sichuan Provincial People's Government.

With over ten captivating books, including *Sanxingdui*, *Tianmen*, *Splendor of Ancient Shu*, and *Golden Sands of Ancient Shu*, Huang Jianhua has explored the fascinating history and culture of ancient China. His full-length novel, *Sorrow and Joy*, and other works, such as *Dreaming of Ancient Shu*, *Legend of the Golden Sands*, and *Lament of Wuding*, transport readers to a bygone era filled with wonder and intrigue. Beyond his engaging prose, Huang Jianhua has also published over 100 academic papers. As a member of the 9th and 10th CPPCC of Sichuan Province, he is dedicated to preserving and sharing the rich heritage of this ancient land.